AF560094

Artisan Industry and Rural Development

Artisan Industry and Rural Development

By

Dr. M. Lakshmi Narasaiah
M.A., Ph.D.
Professor of Economics,
Co-ordinator, Department of M.B.A. and Commerce,
Special Officer,
Sri Krishnadevaraya University Post-graduate Centre,
Kurnool–518 002
Andhra Pradesh (India)

Dr. P. Sreenivasa Naidu,
M.A., M.Phil., Ph.D.
Lecturer in Economics,
Silver Jubilee Government Degree College,
Kurnool–518 002
Andhra Pradesh (India)

DISCOVERY PUBLISHING HOUSE
NEW DELHI

First Published–2006

ISBN: 81-8356-100-4

Published by:

DISCOVERY PUBLISHING HOUSE

4831/24, Prahlad Street, Ansari Road, Darya Ganj
New Delhi–110 002 (India)
Phone: 23279245, • Fax: 91-11-23253475
e-mail: dphtemp@indiatimes.com

Printed at
Arora Offset Press
Laxmi Nagar, Delhi–92

Preface

The planners of most countries have regarded industrialization as the panacea for the development and progress of the country. Development of small scale sector has been important in India because small scale units require less capital outlay and at the same time, provide more employment than the large scale sector. A Small Scale Unit does not require highly sophisticated technology. Apart from their inherent usefulness in terms of numerical superiority, Small Scale Industries play a vital role in the economic growth of developing countries. A study of the Indian Industrial Policy documents reveal that the Small Scale Industrial units have been assigned an important role through out the period since Indian Political Independence.

Artisan Industries: One of the basic objectives of development planning in recent years is improvement of the standards of living of the weaker sections of the community. The artisans and craftsmen who constitute a significant proportion of the weaker sections among the industrial population in rural and semi-urban areas have received due attention.

As a matter of fact, the thrust of the new economic policy is promotion of cottage and handicraft industries as a means, among others, of generating full employment and higher income among the artisans.

Our interest in the present study is basically in the socio-economic conditions of the artisans. An appropriate way of looking at all the levels.of living of these artisans is first to see how they have reacted to the economic stimuli of changes in price and technology. It is also proposed to examine the operation of the institutions build around the artisans in this study.

Dr. M. Lakshmi Narasaiah

Contents

1

Present Study-Scope and Limitations of the Study

The Present Study

In a vast country like India with varied resource base and socio-economic conditions macro level studies may not throw much light on the problems of all regions. So, more micro level studies for each region are necessary for understanding the prospects and problems of artisan units in different regions of our country. The present study conducted in Kurnool District, one of the drought prone and backward districts of Andhra Pradesh, is a modest attempt in this direction and it throws much light on the problems and prospects of artisans and village industrial units in the District.

Who is an Artisan

The Reserve Bank of India declared certain ingredients to consider a person as an artisan depending upon his profession in which he is mainly engaged. The following occupations make it clear.

1. Weavers, Knitters etc.
2. Shoe makers and other leather workers.
3. Dress makers
4. Blacksmith, goldsmith, and other metal workers.
5. Carpenters, painters etc.

6. Stone carvers, brick layers, plasterers, cement finishers etc.
7. Printers (Paper and Textiles) engravers, block makers etc.
8. Potters, glass and ceramic workers etc.
9. Makers of musical instruments, toys, sports goods etc.
10. Basket and mat weavers and related workers.

Therefore, an artisan is a skilled worker in a traditional village craft who works on his own account.[1]

A number of artisans who assisted agriculturists indirectly such as, a carpenter, a blacksmith, a potter, a cobbler, a weaver etc. severely suffered with the advent of Industrial Revolution and subsequent supply of cheap machine made goods and with changes in the habits and tastes of the people. Moreover, with the decay of urban artisan industries, the pressure on land has been increasing. Thus the gradual decline and death of so many traditional industries affected the demographic equilibrium of the Indian population. The number of dependants on Agriculture which was 60 per cent of the total population at the turn of the 18th Century grew to 75 per cent in 1931[2]. Hundreds and Thousands of people who once earned their livelihood from cottage industries were now forced to turn to the over-crowded sector of agriculture to ekeout a meager living as agriculture labourers.

Review of the Literature

Some studies have been undertaken on various programmes and incentives to small industries promotional activities of DICs and problems associated with the implementation of the promotional institutions and the problems faced by the entrepreneurs. SIET (1972)[3] in its study on Hire-purchase has observed that the growth in the number of units and the expansion of capital intensity alone may not create the necessary impetus to the growth unless considerable productivity changes have also been effected through fuller capacity utilisation. Most of the units utilising full capacity have been either big export-oriented industries or local-need-based activities.

The reasons for this under utilisation were mostly insufficient demand for inadequate financial resources for working capital. In a study a spatial diversification of manufacturing industries in Uttar Pradesh, Papola (1979)[4], while furnishing evidence of a continued spatial concentration has noted a decline in the share of factory employment in five most industrialised districts from 57 per cent in 1960 to 55 per cent in 1975 and also in 10 industrially least developed areas from 1.10 per cent to 0.56 per cent. He has concluded that there is a need for a small degree of dispersal of manufacturing activity in favour of backward areas with some degree of industrialisation. Malgaweker (1973)[5] in his study of problems of small industry in Andhra Pradesh has found the lack of infrastructure as a general problems. The industrial estates alone cannot overcome the locational disadvantages. The infrastructural facilities were either very weak or non-existent in rural areas. In Urban areas, with necessary industrial climate and infrastructure facilities, the growth of industries was relatively faster. The scarcity of indigenous raw materials has been a serious bottleneck. Scarce raw materials supplied through quotas were not sufficient to meet the demands of the units. There were delays in the disbursement of the loans due to the existence of procedural delays and instance of tangible securities.

The development of Small Industry also depends on the size of market which in turn depends partly on the efficiency of the size of market which in turn depends partly on the efficiency of the distribution of machinery. It is observed that there was a time lag between sales and realisation of sale proceeds and this affected production of the enterprise.

This study has also found that the incentives provided by the state and the centre were not within the reach of all the entrepreneurs in rural areas.

Andhra Pradesh Industrial Technical Consultancy Organisation (A.P.I.T.C.O.) and Kerala Industrial Technical Consultancy Organisation (K.I.T.C.O.) (1980)[6] conducted a study of the various problems faced by the industries in three states viz., Kerala, Karnataka and Andhra Pradesh. The study revealed that the serious problem faced by the units was the inadequacy of working capital. 69 per cent of units in Kerala, 44 per cent of units in Karnataka and 52 per cent of units in Andhra Pradesh were facing the same problem. The next serious problem was marketing as 30 per cent of the units of Kerala felt it as another setback. Non-availability of raw materials has affected the productivity of several units in all the states especially, in industry groups such as metal-products in Kerala, Chemicals, Rubber and Plastics and metal products in Karnataka, machinery and parts, metal products and chemicals in Andhra Pradesh. It was observed, that the delay in getting timely finance also hampered the productivity of the units and this led to high cost of production, as observed in a few cases, in all the states.

Sarma (1982)[7] who made a study on growth and problems of Small-Scale Sector in Andhra Pradesh, has observed that the backward districts of the State improved their relative positions in terms of units employment and capital during 1966-75. Majority of the small units are confronted with the problems of raw materials and finance.

Sekhar (1983)[8] in his study has observed that the location policies were successful in narrowing the disparities of industrial location in different states. The value added and employment were more equally distributed among the states during 1960 and 1975 as measured by the Theirs inequality and the Harschman Hirfindhal's indices. He also examined intra-regional distribution of industry by comparing the degree of concentration of industrial employment in 1961 and 1971 by grouping cities by size and arrived at the conclusion that, for India as a whole, the degree of concentration of employment in household industry has declined substantially between 1961 and 1971. However, the non-house hold industry maintained its level of concentration during the period.

Rajula Devi (1984)[9] in her study made on the evaluation of Rural industries Project Programme found the following serious deficiencies (i) Some part of the assistance was provided to relatively larger amongst small-scale units, (ii) Assistance was diverted to towns which were excluded from the preview of the scheme (iii) Rural artisans did not receive adequate credit. Indian Institute of Management 1988)[10] in its study conducted on "Evaluation of DIC programme in Andhra Pradesh observed that the General Manager, DIC, as Secretary to the single window committee is expected to hasten up the processing of entrepreneurial cases and thus help the minimisation of delay. Single Window Committee just recommends and requests for speedier action and the DIC have no powers to hasten up and clean up such delayed cases.

Several entrepreneurs in every DIC have been annoyed to find their cases long pending with developmental agencies and local bodies due to indifferent attitude and lack of emphathetic understanding of entrepreneurial problems. With regard to the activities like term loan assistance, working capital assistance, capital subsidy, land and factory shed, many entrepreneurs seemed to have received the requisite help from DIC. In these activities, DICs have mostly recommending powers. For raw materials and other information DICs seem to be playing a very small role.

DICs have been functioning for over a decade since their inception. The above studies have tried to indicate certain deficiencies of various schemes including District Industries Centres but they have not evaluated the performance of DIC at a regional level. Hence, it is time to undertake an evaluative study which is are-specific since India is a vast country with varied socio-economic conditions.

Bhagavati Committee[11] opposes fast introduction of mechanisation designed to replace human labour but, at the same time, recommends introduction of sophisticate technology in certain areas. The Committee recommends reduction to the maximum extent possible in the installed capacity in various industries in order to generate employment in the industrial field. The committee virtually favours creation of employment at any cost without going into the economics of the scheme.

In a study on rural industrialisation in India Bepin Behari[12] examined the problems, possibilities and perspectives of rural industrialisation and discussed the crisis in Indian villages and the need for the new strategy of rural industrialisation and the provision of fuller employment in rural and small-scale industries and technologies. He traced out agricultural development encouragement to village and small-scale industries and general awareness for incorporating appropriate technologies as principal sources of impetus to the programme of technological transformation in rural India. Further he reviewed various measures taken by the Government towards rural industrialisation, local industrial growth, agro based industries, mini-rural cement plants, utilisation of annual waste and harnessing of natural power.

K.V. Bhanuja[13] has suggested that appropriate technology should be developed to promote the rural small industries, N.V. Ratnam[14] opines that infrastructure development for industrialisation in the rural areas and investment in basic services designed to realise the full potential of the human resources in the rural areas should receive a high priority.

Gunnar Myrdal[15] has recommended the adoption of a strategy based on predominantly labour intensive techniques for creating capital and production. The line of approach has been followed up by Sen[16] Johnson[17] Vinod Vysasulu[18] and Raj Krishan[19] suggesting the need for the adoption of an employment-oriented strategy of industrialisation to absorb the rural labour force.

Tin Begen[20] opines that strategy of industrialisation should lay emphasis on labour intensive industries which will create more employment and maximise income. He suggests the adoption of labour-intensive but reasonable efficient techniques. Gautam Mathur[21] opines that the appropriate techniques in the consumption-goods sector will be of a low degree of mechanisation creating incidentally a lot of employment per unit of investment of scarce capital. Dr. Wu, Jageh[22] in his study pointed out that both the capital output ratio and wage-capital ratio show an inverse relationship with capital intensity. He recommends the setting up of SSI in countries having large unemployment. A.C. Minocha[23] has suggested that the strategy of employment-oriented industrialisation should aim at the development of SSI in rural areas.

K.M. Rastogi[24] in his study suggests that the SSI should make use of the indigenous resources in an optimal manner. UNIDO's[25] study indicates that the small enterprises with low-level of investment per worker tend to achieve a higher productivity of capital. The Committee[26] on the village and SSI in its report has stressed that the setting up of SSI will provide employment to the people in rural areas.

K.M. Rastogi[27] has also made a case study of Madhya Pradesh which he calls a Unique case of growing unemployment and poverty amidst plenty. He is in favour of only Small-Scale and Village Industries which make optimum use of indigenous resources and techniques. According to him, there are hundreds of items which can be produced in rural and Small-Scale Industrial units more economically than in a large sector.

Bhagavati[28] Committee opposes fast introduction of mechanisation designed to replace human labour but, at the same time recommends introduction of sophisticated technology in certain select areas. The Committee recommends reduction to the maximum extent possible in the installed-capacity in various industries in order to generate employment in the industrial field. The Committee virtually favour creation of employment at any cost without going into economics of the scheme.

Scope and Limitations of the Study

- the study has covered only 100 artisan units located in Kurnool District;
- only five categories of artisan units are considered for the study;
- the focus of study is category-wise rather than area wise; and
- the study mainly concentrates on the socio-economic conditions, capital structure, employment, cost, sales and marketing problems and prospects of sample units.

On account of limitations, the conclusions arrived at in the present study may not be applicable to other parts of the country, as India is a vast country with regional variations in research endowments, entrepreneurial talents, infrastructural facilities and socio-economic conditions.

Objectives

The main objectives of the present study are:

- to analyse the structural characteristics of the capital of the artisans and village industrial units;
- to examine the employment, capital structure and output in artisan units;
- to identify the operational problems and prospects of artisan and village industrial units;
- to study the financial requirements of the respondents; and
- to analyse whether the finance provided by the Government is adequate to meet the needs of respondents.

Hypotheses

In view of the above objectives the following Hypotheses are formulated:

There is no significant difference in the Socio-Economic status of the beneficiaries in terms of income and asset position;

Given the level of Technology and capital, the artisans maximise their returns by producing to the full capacity and selling their product in the competitive market;

Maximisation of returns depends upon their access to the input market on the one hand and the output market on the other; and

Whether the access enjoyed by any one group of artisans is dependent on the nature of production and market relations and distribution of resources and power among them.

This hypothesis suggests that the economic conditions of the artisan as reflected in his ability to optimise output levels is largely dependent on his Social Status and his place in the power hierarchy.

Methodology

Data Base

Random sampling method has been adopted for this study. Data for the study has been collected from both primary and secondary sources. Secondary sources include census reports, plan documents of Central and State Governments, Financial Institutions, District Industrial Centre and Statistical Abstracts of India and Andhra Pradesh. Primary data has been collected from sample artisan and village industrial units through a schedule constructed for the purpose.

Sample Design

Since the number of artisan units are too large to carry out a census enumeration, adequate data are not easily available. There are 17,883 artisan units in the study area. So, simple random sampling method has been used for the present study. The selected units operating in Kurnool District represent five types of Artisan Category Units. Totally 100 sample units in all the five categories are selected for the study. Thus the sample size for the study is confined to 100 units as detailed in the Table 1.1.

Table 1.1: Category-wise Distribution of Sample Units

Sl. No.	*Artisan Category*	*Total No. of Units Available*	*No. of Sample Units*
1.	Carpentry	2137	20
2.	Blacksmith	1247	20
3.	Cobblery	1771	20
4.	Bamboo Basket Making	2285	20
5.	Goldsmith	1248	20
	Total	8688	100

Source: D.I.C., Kurnool.

Collection of Data

A Schedule is specially prepared for this purpose. The schedule consists of 10 parts, each dealing with the relevant information required for the study. The first part of the schedule deals with the identification and general background of the sample respondent. The second part concentrates on the investment and the sources of finance, the third part focuses on the employment opportunities and working conditions of the hired labour. The fourth part discusses the production and problems in the process of production. The fifth is concerned with the cost. The sixth part treats sales and marketing. The seventh part consist of the artisans and the sources of raw materials. The eighth part is about marketing. The ninth part spotlights the Government policies, regarding artisan units. The last one winds up with the additional and general information regarding artisan units.

The Investigator has administered the schedule among the respondents through personal interviews. As most of them are illiterates, the research worker has to establish a good rapport with the families of the respondents to elicit proper, relevant and correct information. The researcher has made use of the good offices of a number of prominent people in Kurnool District, such as Social Workers, District Industrial Centre Officials etc. to get the required and relevant data for the present study.

Further, the investigator has interviewed the leaders among the artisans and educated people to obtain necessary statistical data for the purpose of study. The information thus collected is supplemented by personal observations of the investigator at the time of collection of field data.

Respondents

Respondents are drawn from all the caste groups in all the parts of Kurnool District. The respondents belong to economically backward castes, backward castes and scheduled caste groups, and scheduled tribes. In case of carpentry the number is large. After enumerating and identifying the artisans in the whole Kurnool district the respondents are selected. Thus the selection of respondents is made taking Kurnool district as a single unit. This is done so because the beneficiaries are not distributed evenly in all the parts of the district. In some parts their number is more and in others their number is marginal (or) negligible.

All the respondents, to whatever caste group they belong, are very poor. They are struggling hard to eke out a decent living. They are very backward from the socio-economic point of view. Their livelihood is earned through their artistic work. The plight of artisans is very deplorable. They are a separate class by themselves in the present social hierarchy and they are suffering a lot due to decline in demand for their trades and products.

Chapterisation (or) Plan of the Book

The present book is divided into six chapters. Introducing the subject, the first chapter depicts the present study, scope and limitations of the study and methodology. The Second chapter consists of Introduction and Role of Artisan in Rural Development. The Third Chapter projects profile of the Kurnool district. The fourth chapter reveals the implementation of Adarana Scheme for rural artisans in Kurnool district. The fifth chapter reflects the socio-economic conditions of artisans in Kurnool district. The Sixth chapter gives a summary of the entire work taken up by the author on one hand and on the other gives suggestions to improve the living and working conditions of the artisans.

REFERENCES

1. M.A. Oommen Banks in the Service of Weaker Section, pp. 6-7.
2. Marks and Engles on COLONIALISM, pp. 117-120.
3. Small Industries Extension Training (SIET). A Study of National Small Industries Corporation is Hire Purchases Scheme, Hyderabad SIET Institute, March, 1972.
4. People, T.S., Spatial Diversification of Manufacturing Industries in Uttar Pradesh, Lucknow, Giri Insititute of Development Studies, 1979.
5. Malgawakar, P.D., "Problems of Small Industry, A study in Andhra Pradesh". Hyderabad, SIET, 1973.
6. Andhra Pradesh Industrial Technical Consultancy Organisation and Kerala Industries Technical Consultancy Organisation. "Survey of Industrial Estates in India. Semion Industrial Development of Backwards Areas, sponsored by Industrial Development Bank of India, May 7, 1980.
7. Sarma, R.K. Industrial Development of Andhra Pradesh. A Regional Analysis, Bombay, Himalaya Publishing House, 1982.
8. Sekhar, A., Uday, Industrial Location Policy-The Indian experience, World Bank Staff working paper No. 620, Washington, 1983.
9. Devi Rajula "Industrialisation Holds Key to Rural Development Kurukshetra, December, 1984, 0.34.

10. Indian Institute of Management, Evaluation of DIC Programme Andhra Pradesh, Bangalore, May, 1988.

11. Government of India. Report of the Committee on Unemployment (Bhagavati Committee, New Delhi) (1973).

12. Bepin Behari. Rural Industrialisation in India. Vikas Publishing House, New Delhi (1976).

13. Banujam, K.V. (1996), Poverty Alleviation through Rural Industrialisation, Kurukshetra (India's Journal of Rural Development) Vol.XXXIII No.1 October, (1984) p.p. 51-53.

14. Rathnam, N.V. (1984). Rural Industrialisation and IRDP Kurukshetra (India's Journal of Rural Development) Vol. XXXIII No. 3, December, 1984) pp. 4-8.

15. Myrdal Gunnar: Asian Drama, An Enquiry into the Poverty of Nations, the Penguin Press, London. (1968).

16. Sen, A.K., Employment, Technology and Development, Oxford. (1975).

17. Johnson Harry, G., Technology and Economic Interdependence. (1975).

18. Vyasulu Vinod (1976). Technology and Change in Underdeveloped Societies Economic and Political Weekly, August, 28 (1975).

19. Raj Krishna. Rural Unemployment Policies for the Fifth Plan, Economic and Political Weekly, March, 3. (1973).

20. Tin Bergen, J. Discussion in Manar Hada (ED) Problems of Unemployment in India, Allied Publishers, p. 7.

21. Mathur, Gautam, True Employment and Non Employment in D.L. Narayana et. al., (Eds), Planning for Employment, Sterling Publishers, (1980) pp. 1-9.

22. Wu, Jageh, Capital Intensity and Economic Growth under Developed Countries. Ising Hua Journal of Chinese Studies, New Series, III-IV (1968) pp 219-245.

23. Minocha, A.C. Industrial Development in M.P. Regional Structure and Strategy for Employment Oriental Industrialisation in D.L. Narayana et. al., (Eds) O. Peit (1980) pp. 259-307.

24. Rastogi, K.M., Employment Generation through S.S.V. and C.I.A. case study of M.P. in D.L. Narayana et. al., (Eds), op cit, pp. 308-320.

25. UNIDO SSI in LAIN America, Publication No. 111337, (1969) p. 56.

26. Government of India, Planning Commission (1956). Report of the Committee on Village and SSI (Chairman), D.G. Karve).

27. Rastogi, K.M., Employment Generation through S.S. Village and Cottage Industries, A case study of M.P. in D.L. Narayan et al., (Eds). (1980).

28. Government of India, Report of the Committee on unemployment (Bhagavati Committee). New Delhi. (1973).

2

Introduction and Role of Artisans in Rural Development

Development of the poor like rural artisans depends upon several factors. It is not just a question of Internal cultural variations but external physical variations also contribute to their development. The various forms of stimuli which the artisans receive should therefore be both internal and external.

Artisans have a vital role to play in the economic development of the country. They have certain inherent basic skills, which, if identified and harnessed would usher in a new era. The Government of India and the State Governments have realized this role of the artisans, who are a part of the general poor class and as such suffer from certain socio-economic handicaps. Several millions of rupees have been spent by the Government while implementing the Five Year Plans. A number of developmental variables have been included. These variables are both economic and non-economic. Economic variables centre around employment opportunities, roads, water, electricity, transport and communications etc. Socio-cultural variables related to education, medical facilities, social organisation, leadership etc.

All these years, the focus had been on making out some financial help and leaving everything to the people themselves and to the bureaucrats. But for various reasons such a strategy did not bear the expected results. Hence the new strategy adopted was to make people participate in developmental activities as partners. The change agents and change targets had to have close and cordial network of social relationship. Hence more and more scope is now available for such relationship which could bring about social transformation.

Another significant change noticed today is that instead of local efforts for development, there are also global efforts. We are witnessing the metamorphosis of the whole world into a family. Many developed countries have realized that they have a mission to serve the poor wherever they are, irrespective of territorial, religious and racial considerations. This spontaneous intervention is often well planned and hence positive results are expected.

Artisans traditionally belonged to the professions of blacksmithy, carpentry, cobblery, bamboo basket making, goldsmithy, pottery, weaving and oil extraction etc., According to 2001 census there were 15 million artisans in the country. At least the small and marginal farmers have some durable assets namely, land. Most artisans do not have even this vital asset. The main asset of the artisans is certain skills they possess such as basket making, shoe-making etc., In most cases these skills are learnt traditionally. It is obvious that unless efforts are made to help artisans develop economically, they will be forced to work as agricultural labourers or to join the ranks of the rural unemployed.

Need for Industrialisation in Developing Countries

Over the years, the Governments of developing countries have adopted positive measures to defeat the forces of stagnation. To perform this gigantic task, a well-considered and most suited policy of economic development has been framed. The growth process of these countries aims at accelerating the economic development to enhance social welfare. In fact, the economic change is a part of a wider social change and the economic development is a long-term process of intrinsic growth. Therefore, the task of policy making has a vital role to play in selecting the desired objectives and suitable alternatives for stimulating the economic growth. It also requires a careful examination of the existing institutional framework, social values, economic requirements and their implications, keeping in view, the need for rapid social and economic development of the economy.

Now-a-days, most of the developing countries are following the thesis that industrialisation is a process of growth and as such is organically linked both to the social and economic past and to the parallel processes of social and economic development[1]. The thesis reaffirms the importance of industrialisation as an effective means for solving the problems of economic and social backwardness in developing countries of the world.

Since the end of the Second World War, most of the developing countries have been giving top priority to industrialisation. Actually, the planners of most of the developing countries have regarded industrialisation as the panacea for underdevelopment and poverty. The most primitive economies are now keenly interested in rapidly enlarging manufacturing industry. It is in rapid industrialisation "in which they place a major hope of finding a solution to their problems of poverty, insecurity, over-population and ending their newly realised backwardness in the modern world.[2]

The poor countries believe that industrialisation brings some basic changes in the production-functions and techniques, occupational structure and the level of activities in different sectors of the economy. These changes will remove the obstacles which retard the growth, and will raise the standard of living. Gunnar Myrdal has rightly pointed out the relationship of industrialisation to economic development when he observed that "the manufacturing industry represents, in a sense, a higher stage of production in advanced countries." The development of manufacturing has been concomitant with spectacular economic progress and rise in the levels of living in these countries. In the underdeveloped countries too, the productivity in industry tends to be considerably greater than in the traditional agricultural pursuits.

In the light of the aforesaid facts, it cannot be denied that industrialisation, in general, can be the best means of achieving the higher growth rate and raising the living standards of the people. In the context of the developing economies, a few specific objects and policies of industrialisation have been generally agreed on by the planners. They are to provide work for growing populations, to raise the standard of living by increasing the per capita income, net national income and often to improve balance of payments situations."[3] So it can be deduced that the development of small-scale industries also can provide large-scale employment to the growing population in developing countries.

Role of Small Scale Industries in Industrialisation

India is often described as an underdeveloped country. The term underdeveloped implies that the resources of the country both human and material—have not been properly harnessed and as a result the people are compelled to live in poverty. They are underfed and physically weak and their working capacity is low. 'Underdevelopment' implies that the level of real income and per capita income is low as judged by the standards in developed countries of North America and Western Europe. In underdeveloped countries, there is no large-scale application of the fruits of scientific and technological advances to agriculture and industry. Subsistence production is generally important enough to the people here, the markets are comparatively narrow and manufacturing industry is usually unimportant.[4]

In many developing countries, manpower is relatively abundant. It is, therefore, imperative that their full and effective utilisation should become a focal point of socio-economic policies. Emphasis has to be laid on small scale industries to absorb the surplus manpower in these countries.

The concept of small scale industry covers a wide range of activities and its definition changes from time to time. The latest definition (Feb' 1997) of small scale industries is quite broad based. All industries with a capital investment of Rs. 75 Lakhs in plant and machinery are classified as small scale industries. The smaller units with a capital investment of Rs. 2 Lakhs in plant and machinery are classified as tiny units. Units with a capital investment in plant and machinery varying between Rs. 20 Lakhs and Rs. 25 Lakhs are classified as ancillary industries.

The development of small scale sector has been important in India because of the following reasons: First, the small scale units require less capital outlay and at the same time, they provide more employment than the large scale sector. Second, a small scale unit does not require highly sophisticated technology. It can, therefore, be useful in backward areas where the people have yet to be trained to meet the challenge of sophisticated technology.

Importance of Small Scale Industries

Apart from their inherent usefulness in terms of numerical superiority, small scale industries play a vital role in the economic growth of developing countries as discussed below:

Utilisation of Resources

Small Scale Industries facilitate the tapping of resources which otherwise would remain unused. These resources include entrepreneurship, capital labour and raw materials. They can mobilize rural savings which may otherwise remain idle or may be spent on luxuries or channelled into non-productive ventures.

Employment Generation

Since they are fairly labour-intensive, small-scale industries create employment opportunities at a relatively low-capital cost. In India, there is a basic problem of absorbing the surplus manpower in non-agricultural jobs and providing additional employment opportunities to the growing population.

Generation of Foreign Exchange

Small-Scale industries facilitate substantial foreign exchange savings and earnings. A wide range of consumable and simple goods, which are now being imported, can be economically produced on a small scale basis if adequate facilities are provided to the small scale industries across the country.

Diversification of Industrial Structures

Small Scale Industries contribute significantly to the strengthening of the industrial structure. Many more articles can be produced economically by the small scale than the large scale industries.

Entrepreneurial Development

Small Scale Industries serve as seedbeds of entrepreneurship. They serve the developing economy not only by their output of goods but also by functioning as a nursery to entrepreneurial and managerial talent. This role of small scale industries is of decisive importance in any economy where the industrial structure consists of a few large scale and medium sized industries, on the one hand and large number of traditional industries such as artisan units, handicrafts and cottage industries on the other.

Regional Development and Industrial Dispersal

The concentration of industrial and other activities has given birth to the phenomenon of the so called pockets of development where economic and social change is achieved at much faster rate than in the outlaying rural districts.

This trend of uneven development, although predominant, can be checked and corrected through the establishment of small scale industries. For one thing, such industries lead to the creation of employment opportunities on a dispersed basis not only in large cities and towns but also in small towns and so wide spread establishment of small scale industries would, make it possible to reverse the current trend of the migration of the people from rural to urban areas.

Small Scale Industry and Industrial Policy Resolutions

A study of the industrial policy documents reveals that small scale industry unit has been assigned an important role throughout the period since Indian political independence. Thus, for example protection and promotion of small scale industry has long been listed as a major objective in all of the industrial policy documents. The policy statements also indicate the lines on which the Government has been taking, or contemplating, concrete steps.

The point may be highlighted by referring to the Industrial Policy Resolutions.

Industrial Policy Resolution, 1948

This Policy Resolution of 1948 recognises the fact that cottage and small scale industries have a very important role in the national economy, offering much scope to individual, village or cooperative enterprise and serving as means for the rehabilitation of displaced persons. These industries are particularly suited for the better utilisation of local resources and for the achievement of local self sufficiency in respect of certain types of essential consumer goods like food, cloth and agricultural implements. Healthy expansion of cottage and small scale industries depends upon a number of factors like the provision of raw materials, cheap power, technical advice, organised marketing of their produce, and wherever necessary, safeguards against the intensive competition by large scale manufacture, and as on the education of the workers in the use of the best available techniques.

Industrial Resolution, 1956

This Resolution Policy of the Government of India of 1956 stresses the role of cottage, village and small scale industries in the development of the national economy. In relation to some of the problems that need urgent solutions the small scale industries offer some distinct advantages. They provide immediate large scale employment. They offer a method of ensuring a more equitable distribution of the national income and facilitate an effective mobilisation of resources of capital and skill which might otherwise remain unutilised. Some of the problems that unplanned urbanisation tend to create will be avoided by the establishment of small centres of industrial production all over the country.

The Government of India has been following a policy of supporting cottage and small scale industries by restricting the volume of production in the large scale sector, by differential taxation or by direct subsidies. While such measures continue to be taken, whenever necessary, the aim of the State Policy will be to ensure that the decentralised sector acquires sufficient strength to support its development integrated with that of large scale industry.

Industrial Policy Resolution, 1977

The importance assigned to small scale industry is emphasised in a still greater measure in the 1977, Industrial Policy Resolution.

The emphasis of Industrial Policy before the adoption of Industrial Policy Resolution was mainly on large industries neglecting cottage industries completely or giving a minor role to them. The firm policy of the Government was to change this approach. The main aim of the new industrial policy was the effective promotion of cottage and small scale industries widely dispersed in rural areas and small towns.

From the greater emphasis laid on the small scale industry by 1977 Resolution, a big imputes has been given to the growth of the decentralised sector. Thus, for example the items reserved for this sector have been increased to cover 504 instead of 180. Since then the number has been further increased and expanded to 807 items. The statement also declares the intention of the Government to provide maximum support to the small scale industries for product standardisation, quality control, marketing etc., on priority basis. Within the small scale sector a sub sector of tiny units has been created and this sub sector is expected to receive a preferential treatment even within the small scale sector.

It was also proposed in the statement to enact special legislation for protecting the interest of cottage and household industries, with each district having one agency called the "District Industries Centre" to deal with the requirements of this industry. A separate wing was to be created in the Industrial Development Bank of India for Small Scale Industries to provide effective financial support to this sector. Finally special measures were envisaged for modernising khadi and village industries and for promoting appropriate technologies all around.

Industrial Policy Resolution, 1980

The Industrial Policy Statement made by Government of India on 23rd July, 1980 primarily sought to harmonise the growth in the small scale sector with that in the large and medium sectors. The emphasis in the new policy was on fostering the complementarity between the large and small sectors so that the new dichotomies (which are more on paper than real) between the two sectors would not distort the economic pattern.

The broad socio-economic objectives of the New Industrial Policy of 1980 were set out as follows:[5]

- optimum utilisation of installed capacity;
- maximising production and achieving higher productivity;
- higher employment generation;
- correction of regional imbalances through a preferential development of industrially backward areas;

- strengthening of the agricultural base by according a preferential treatment to agro based industries and promoting optimum intersectorial relationship;
- faster promotion of export oriented and import substitution industries;
- promoting economic federalism with an equitable spread of investment and the dispersal of return amongst widely spread small but growth units in rural as well as urban areas; and
- consumer protection against high prices and bad quality.

An important element of the new policy was the raising of the investment limits of the tiny and small scale sectors. These limits were redefined in terms of investment in plant and machinery and were fixed as Rs. 2 Lakhs for tiny sector instead of Rs. 1 Lakh, Rs. 20 Lakhs for the small scale sector instead of Rs. 10 Lakhs and Rs. 25 Lakhs instead of Rs. 15 Lakhs for ancillaries. This step was essentially a pragmatic one, and took into account the significant price rise that occurred in the last five years following the fixation of the investment limits for the small scale sector.

This decision would, it was hoped, bring into the fold of the small scale sector, a number of technology oriented units, whose growth would be backed by a suitable system of incentives. The new industrial policy spelt out some of these incentives which were proposed to be provided so that the small scale sector might grow in a significant measure and contribute to the national economy.

The policy statement of 1980 made it clear that the existing support programme for marketing as well as the reservation of items in the small scale sector would continue. The basic thrust of this policy was to ensure a continuous growth of the small scale sector without inhibiting the growth of other sectors. In this context, automatic growth for a large number of industries in the medium and large sector would be ensured so that they could grow without hindrance.

A special emphasis was laid on the establishment of 'nucleus plants' in backward districts around which a programme of ancillarisation would be developed. A quote from the statement: "The proposed nucleus plants in industrially backward district would generate a net work of small scale units or the existing network of small scale units in an area would acquire a faster growth by the coming up of a nucleus plant in the area. In between the nucleus large plants and the satellite ancillaries the Government would permit a system of linkages for an integrated industrial development[6]. The new policy targets set for the sixth plan are production of the value of more than Rs. 35,000 Crores, employment of 11 million persons and promotion of exports totalling nearly Rs. 2,000 Crores. The small scale sector might look forward to a steady and balanced growth within the framework of the new policy statement of the Government of India."

Industrial Policy, 1990

The Government has been considering the need to take measures for promotion of small scale, and agro-based, industries and to change procedures for grant of industrial approvals.

1. *Main objectives:* In pursuance of Industrial Policy to re-orient industrial growth to serve the objectives of employment generation, dispersal of industry in rural areas and to enhance the contribution of small scale industries to exports, it has been decided to take the measures enumerated below.

2. *Investment Ceiling for Small Scale and Ancillary Units:* The investment ceiling in plant and machinery for small scale industries (fixed in 1985) would be raised from the present Rs. 35 Lakhs to Rs. 60 Lakhs and correspondingly, for ancillary units, from Rs. 45 Lakhs

to Rs. 75 Lakhs. In order to enable small scale industries to play an important role in the total export effort, the small scale units which undertake to export at least 30 per cent of the annual production by the third year will be permitted to step up their investment in plant and machinery to Rs. 75 Lakhs.

3. *Tiny Units:* Investment ceiling in respect of tiny units would also be increased from the present Rs. 2 Lakhs to Rs. 5 Lakhs. However, with regard to their locations, the population limit of 50,000 as per 1981 census would continue to apply. Steps will be taken to ensure better inflow of credit and other vital inputs and to improve infrastructural support to the constituents of the tiny sector.

4. *Reservation Items:* Presently, 836 items have been reserved for exclusive manufacture in the small scale sector. Efforts will be made to identify more items for similar reservation. Encroachment and violation by large scale units into areas, reserved for small scale sector will be effectively dealt with.

5. *Central Investment Subsidy:* A new scheme of central investment subsidy exclusively for the small scale sector in rural and backward areas capable of generating higher level of employment at lower capital cost would be implemented.

6. *Upgradation of Technology:* With a view to improving the competitiveness of the products manufactured in the small scale sector, programmes for modernisation and upgradation of technology would be implemented. A number of technology centres, tool rooms, process and product development centres, testing centres etc. will be set up under the umbrella of an apex technology development centre in the Small Industries Development Organisation (SIDO).

7. *Flow of Credit:* To ensure adequate and timely flow of credit for Small Scale Industries, a new apex bank

known as Small Industries Development Bank of India (SIDBI) has already been established. One of the major tasks of SIDBI and other Commercial Banks/Financial Institutions would be, to channelise need-based flow of credit, both by way of term loan and working capital to the tiny and rural industries. A targeted approach will be adopted to ensure implementation and to facilitate monitoring this objective.

8. *Review of Fiscal Concessions:* The existing regime of fiscal concessions will be reviewed both to provide sustained support to the units in the small scale sector and to remove the disincentives for their graduation and further growth.

9. *Identification of Locations:* An exercise will be undertaken to identify locations in rural areas endowed with adequate power supply and intensive campaigns will be launched to attract suitable entrepreneurs, to provide all other inputs and foster small scale and tiny industries. Similarly, industries which are not energy intensive will be identified for proliferation in rural areas where power supply is presently a constraint.

10. In order to widen the entrepreneurial base, the Government would lay particular emphasis on training women and youth under the entrepreneurial development programme. A special cell would be established in Small Industries Development Organisation (SIDO) and State Directorate of Industries to assist women entrepreneurs.

11. *Relaxation in Bureaucratic Controls:* One of the persistent complaints of the small scale units is their being subjected to a large number of acts/laws, their being required to maintain a number of registers, submit plethora of returns and face an army of inspectors, particularly in the field of labour legislations. These bureaucratic controls will be reduced so that unnecessary interference is eliminated.

12. *Expansion in Activities of KVIC and KVI Board:* In order to assist the large number of artisans engaged in rural and cottage industries, activities of the Khadi and Village Industries Commission (KVIC) and KVI board will be expanded and these organisations will be strengthened to discharge the duties more effectively. Special marketing organisations at the Central and State levels shall be created to assist rural artisans in marketing their products and also in supply of raw materials. Besides providing concessional credit, training facilities and free consultancy to artisans will be provided.

13. *Agro Processing Industries:* In agro processing industries, greater success has been achieved where growers and processors have been integrated, as in the case of sugar. For the success of other agro-based industries also, close links must be forged between the growers and processor units. Industrial policy will, therefore, especially promote projects which are organised in close co-operation on the basis of joint ownership. Growers will be encouraged to set up processing units within the framework of co-operative societies or similar institutional framework. This will also ensure the transmission of better technology for enhanced agricultural production.

14. In sectors where units require licensing, the policy will also encourage location of processing units in rural areas where growers are concentrated. Apart from economic benefits of proximity to raw materials, it will help in dispersal of industry and increasing employment in rural areas.

15. Agro-processing industry will receive high priority in credit allocation from the financial institutions. In the allotment of working capital, banks will give higher priority to such industries as compared with the rest of the industrial sector.

16. In order to bring the best technology available to these industries, technology approvals will be given within 30 days of presentation to the Secretariat for Industrial Approvals in the Department of Industrial Development. Government will actively promote and generate adoption of new technologies in the field.

17. *Procedures for Industrial Approvals:* Indian industry must be made more competitive internationally. It also needs to be released from unnecessary bureaucratic shackles by reducing the number of clearances required from the Government. While the Government continues to examine large projects in view of resource constraints, decisions in respect of medium sized investments will be left to the entrepreneurs. To achieve these objectives, the following decisions have been taken.

18. *Delicensing:* All new units up to an investment of Rs. 25 crores in fixed assets in no-backward areas and Rs. 75 crores in centrally notified backward areas will be exempted from obtaining licence/registration.

19. *Capital Goods (CG.):* For the import of capital goods, the entrepreneur would have entitlement to import up to a value of 30 per cent of the total value of plant and machinery required for the unit.

20. *Raw Materials and Components:* For import of raw materials and components, imports will be permissible up to a value of 30 per cent of the ex-factory value of annual production. The ex-factory value of production will exclude the excise duty on the item of production.

21. *Foreign Collaboration:* In respect of transfer of technology, if import of technology is considered necessary by the entrepreneur, he can enter into an agreement with the collaborator, without obtaining any clearance from the Government, provided that royalty payment does not exceed 5 per cent on domestic sales and 8 per

cent of exports. If, however, lump sum payment is involved in the import of technology, the proposal will require Government clearance, but a decision will be communicated to the entrepreneur within a period of 30 days.

22. *Foreign Investment:* Keeping in view the need to attract effective inflow of technology, investment up to 40 per cent of equity will be allowed on an automatic basis. In such proposals also, the landed value of imported capital goods shall not exceed 30 per cent of value of plant and machinery.

23. *Minimum Economic Size:* In order to ensure that investment leads to production of goods that attain international competitiveness and that maximum efficiency is ensured. The unit will have to conform to the minimum economic size in cases where such a size has been prescribed.

24. *Expansion:* The de-regulation suggested above, would cover all cases of expansion and would not be restricted only to new units.

25. *Broad Banding:* The existing Broad Banding Scheme would continue to be in force. In addition, if no extra investment is required, no clearance from the Government would be necessary for production and sale of any new item by existing units. This would not include those items which are reserved for small scale industries.

26. *Location Policy and Environmental Clearance:* The location policy would not be applied to such industries by the Centre except for location in and around metropolitan cities where location will not be permissible within 20 km. calculated from the periphery of the metropolitan area except prior designated industrial areas and for – non-polluting industries such as electronics, computer software and printing. It will be up to State Governments to regulate industrial locations keeping in mind local

conditions and requirement and their respective spatial development plans and zoning and town planning laws. Similarly, environmental clearance will have to be obtained from the prescribed authority at the State level. In future, Central legislation should introduce new provisions, so that law would automatically apply to these units as well.

27. *Export Oriented Units:* Hundred per cent export oriented units (EOUs) and units to be set up in export processing zones (EPZs) are also being delicensed under the scheme up to an investment limit of Rs. 75 crores.

28. *Convertibility Clause:* Such investments shall be exempted from the "convertibility clause" applicable to financing by Indian Financial Institutions.

29. It may be clarified that in the application of the proposals for exemption 836 items which are reserved for production in the small scale sector will continue to be excluded.

30. The above proposals will be applicable to all manufactured items in the specified list. The list shall follow the nomenclature of the Indian trade classification based on the harmonised system. In each section of the classification, apart from positive mention of approved items, those not permissible shall be specifically excluded from the benefit of the proposals listed above. Approval for excluded items will be as per the existing industrial policy regime and procedures.

31. Units set up by Monopoly Restricting Trade Practice/ Foreign Exchange Regulation Act. Companies will be covered by the procedures set out above, but they will continue to need clearances under the provisions and regulations of these two acts.

New Industrial Policy, 1991

In line with the liberalisation measures announced during eighties the government announced a New Industrial policy on July 24, 1991. This new policy de-regulates the Industrial economy in a substantial manner. The major objectives of the new policy are to build on the gains already made, correct the distortions or weaknesses that might have crept in, maintain a sustained growth in productive and gainful employment and attain international competitiveness.

Main Objectives

1. *Abolition of Industrial Licensing:* In a major move to liberalise the economy, the new industrial policy abolished all industrial licensing irrespective of the level of investment, except for certain industries related to security and strategic concerns, social reasons, concerns related to safety and overriding environmental issues, manufacture of products of hazardous nature and articles of elitist consumption. Now there are only 7 industries for which licensing is compulsory.

2. *Public Sectors role diluted:* The number of industries reserved for the public sector since 1956 was 17. This number has now been reduced to 6. Among the industries reserved earlier were many core industries like iron and steel, electricity, air transport, ship building, heavy machinery industries such as heavy electrical plants and telecommunication cables and instruments. The new industrial policy has removed all these industries from the reserved list. Industries which continue to be reserved for the public sector are in areas where security and strategic concerns predominate. These areas are 6 in number.

3. *Monopoly Restrictive Trade Practice Limit goes:* The MRTP act has been accordingly amended. The amended act gives more emphasis to the prevention and control of monopolistic restrictive and unfair trade practices so that those consumers are adequately protected from such practices.

4. *Free entry to Foreign Investment and Technology:* As in the case of domestic industrial investment foreign

investment has also been traditionally regulated in India. The industrial policy has prepared a list specifying high technology and high investment priority industries wherein automatic permission will be available for direct foreign investment upto 51 per cent foreign equity.

5. *Industrial Location Policy Liberalised:* In a departure from the prevailing locational policy for industries, the new industries policy provides that in locations other than cities of more than 1 million population, there will be no need of obtaining industrial approvals from the Centre, except for industries subject to compulsory licensing.

6. *Abolition of phased manufacturing programmes for new projects:* To force the pace of indeginisation in manufacturing, phased manufacturing programmes have been in force in a number of engineering and electronic industries. The new industrial policy has abolished such programmes in future as the Government feels that due to substantial reforms made in the trade policy and the devaluation of the rupees, there is no longer any need for enforcing the local content requirements on a case by case administrative basis. Various incentives that are currently available to manufacturing units with existing phased manufacturing programmes will continue.

Rural Industrialisation in India

What is a Rural Industry?

Strictly speaking, no clear definition exits for a rural industry. This can be an off-shoot of the present institutional set up of the industrial scene in India. The existing set up does not have a separate organisation to promote the entire spectrum of rural industries in the country. As a result it is scattered: it comes under different Directorates and Ministries. This itself puts a number of limitations on the availability of secondary data of this sector.[7]

Of course, the industries located in rural areas are rural industries. The Planning Commission first used the term "rural industries" when it recommended a Rural Industries Projects Programme in the year 1962. In a Report on Village and Small Industries Sector, the Planning Commission (1991) defined rural industries in the following way. "The term 'rural industries' connotes such type of industries as Khadi, Village industries, handloom, handicraft, sericulture, coir and tiny and service industries situated in rural areas". This shows that the term "Village and Small Industry" used by the Government generally represents rural industry and it excludes the modern small scale industries located in rural areas. We classify the rural industry broadly into two groups, traditional village industries and modern small scale industries in the rural areas.

A practical approach for this purpose would be to consider all the non urban areas as rural areas. If one looks at the industries in this way, most of the industries that come under the ASI (Annual Survey of Industries) are urban concentrated and undoubtedly have a predominantly urban bias. Though we have a general perception that, any industry concentrated in rural area is a rural industry, certain industries need not be so. The larger size of certain industries, which are supposed to start in urban areas, might have been forced to shift to rural area. And even so with the setting up of the industry in rural places they may turn into urban areas. This is especially so in the case of large public sector units set up on greenfield sites – like, say, NALCO in Koraput district of Orissa. The industries concentrated in urban areas can be considered modern urban industries.

There are several ways of classifying rural industries. One classification is based on the over all role of the sector in the stages of industrial development. They are proto-industries, distress industries and dispersed industries. Proto industries are pre-factory manufacturing in nature, they exist in the dominantly agricultural economies, traditional industries come under this category.[8] The distress industries are a part of the phenomenon of distress diversification, where people are forced to get into some industries which may provide minimum returns needed for survival. In India, most of the traditional industries still may be viewed as distress industries. The third and the most important category, dispersed industries, emerges as part of the real process of industrialisation. These industries are generally found to be efficient. The example is the modern small scale sector in India. Thus, rural industry is a mixture of different types or sizes of industries.

One of the most popular and a very suitable classification for the Indian condition is on the basis of the nature of products, technology and skill existing in these industries. Accordingly, rural industries in India can be classified into traditional and modern. The traditional industry has its origin in the village life and is a mix of artisan industries and traditional crafts. These industries are interwoven with the village life and use traditional technology based on local resources and skills, catering to local village needs (Chadha, 1993). The products in these industries are a part of life, and productivity has only a small place in them. The success in these industries largely depends on "the skill and devotion of the worker and not merely on supplementary factors like tools and implements, and these are less dependent on the social overheads" (Vyas and Mathai, 1978). The present KVI sector can be cited as the best example of these industries. The village or traditional industries are of various types. The most important among them are the KVI, handlooms, coir, handicrafts, cashew processing, tile manufacturing.

One of the main features of the traditional sector is that, it has never been a part of the organised industrial sector of the economy. But, the small scale sector, and the tiny sector, at least for their machine parts and other inputs are connected to the industrial sector (for the historical reasons, see Tyabji, 1989). Thus, most of the traditional industries are poor in forward linkages (Chadha, 1993). In terms of technology, employment conditions, marketing etc., the modern sector stands ahead compared to the traditional sector and the tiny sector. The rest of this paper classifies the rural industry into traditional and non traditional or modern.

The modern small scale industrial sector is a heterogeneous group in itself. It comprises, modern, rural small industries and the tiny rural industries. Compared to the village industries, technology and production conditions are superior in these industries. They create full time employment to the workers. Some of the modern small industries, unlike the traditional industries are concentrated in urban as well as in urban agglomerations.

The Background to the Policy

The post independence era saw diverging views on small industry. The difference had a root in the pre-independence era, it was basically in the form of what may be called Gandhian and Nehruvian views. At the time of independence, the capital concentration reached its maximum level, and industrial production was in the hands of small producers (Tyabji, p.1). Along with this group, there was also the simultaneous existence of one more group called, the traditional craftsmen, who exchanged their produce on a traditional basis. The policy measures taken by the imperial administration were in favour of the capitalist commodity producing class. This class played a significant role in moulding the future industrial policy of the country (for details, see Tyabji).

The Gandhian approach towards small industry was to protect small producers comprising small agricultural industrial producers. It gained much popularity with the national movement. This was supported by the large industrialists mainly because of their fear of the Nehruvian approach to nationalisation and of a dominant public sector. Gandhiji had the conception of a decentralised village economy, which was reflected in the Khadi and Swadeshi movement.

The support given by the Congress Party to handloom that is, cloth woven by hand from mill – spun yarn, was further extension to the support given to two major cottage industries (Tyabji 1991 p. 117). It shows how the Gandhian ideology is worked out through the Congress Party. The Khadi sector represented the poor and landless artisans.

At the same time, there was support to small capitalists mainly to contribute to mitigating unemployment. If we compare this with the post independence policy, the evidence clearly suggests that the Gandhian strategy was not given enough attention. We can see that the small scale industrialisation strategy had a bias towards the capitalist form of development. Of course, the capitalist development was not in any case what the Gandhians wanted – they wanted the supply of consumer goods to come principally from village and cottage industries essentially using traditional technology and no wage labour (Tyabji, 1989).

On the other hand, soon after independence there was a consensus on the strong public sector involvement in the strategic areas. This was mainly the Nehruvian approach. Modern small industries were given a special role in the generation of more employment in the country. This in fact, is reflected in the early five year plan models. This is cited as the basis of the growth of strong public as well as private involvement in the growth of small industry. In general, the policy of the Janata Government in 1977-79 was in line with Gandhian thinking while Congress Policy endorsed the Nehruvian path. Thus, the small industrial policies as such shows a mix in their approach towards these sectors. In the words of Tyabji.

> *"The accepted approach to small units was initially elaborated and subsequently influenced in its development by the operation of the representatives of various socio-economic interests. These interests consisted of elements such as the British capitalists and big and small capitalists, the middle class and rural craftsmen in India (Tyabji, 1989, p.147).*

Were both these sections, with diverging views satisfied by the post independence policies? The answer is no. In fact, the policy makers faced opposition not only from the Gandhian, who disagreed with the capitalist strategy of development, but also from the industrial interests who saw their short or even medium term interests attacked by the State policy of encouraging the rise of new capitalist interests (Tyabji, p. 174). While this continues, as an influence of the above factors, we can see two types of reflections on small scale industrial policy, one is on protection, and the other on promotion. The protectionist polices are largely aimed at protecting the traditional sector, while the promotionist policies wanted to promote small scale industrial growth in the country. Further, the traditional sector became a part of the concern for social welfare and employment generation. Efficiency and productivity became the objectives of the modern small scale sector. We concentrate on these aspects in the following sections.

The Industrial Development and Regulation Act of 1951, laid the base of small scale industry policy in India. The Act, proclaimed the industries which have to be registered, and listed industries in respect of which a licence is required for starting. The Act excluded the small scale sector as well as small factories from registration (The excluded sector later grew as the small scale industry of India). This exclusion might have been the result of a consensus to protect the small industrial capitalist of the country.

> *"Thus, a kind of compromise is visible between the two approaches, representing the views of Gandhi and Nehru. With the First Five Year Plan, one of the objective had been the rapid and widespread development of the small industries, including cottage, household and small scale industries "(L.C. Jain, 1980, P. 1747).*

Rural Industry Policy in India: An overview

The need for policies of small scale, decentralised, regional development stems from two circumstances. The first is inter-regional variations in the availability as well as utilisation of resources required for growth, this leads quite naturally to uneven growth. This happens over a long period of development process. To correct the imbalances arising out of such a growth, decentralised policies are essential. The second comes from a mere increase in the economic production of certain goods and services to improve the general well being of the society.

These two factors together with regional participation, resource endowments and levels of socio-economic development, constitute the basic reason for regional planning and rural industrialisation (Sigurdson, p. 668). Rural industrialisation, thus, is concerned with the spread of industrial units to the rural areas and the growth of village and small scale industries. This is reflected in part in the various Industrial Policy Resolutions of India.

The first Industrial Policy Resolution of 1948, assigned the production of commodities like implements, clothes and other local resource oriented commodity production to the small scale industry. This is reflected in the first five year plan also. These village and small industries were considered a thrust area next to agriculture. In the same plan, a number of special boards were set up for developing specific segments of the traditional sector—namely, Khadi and Village Industries, Handlooms, Handicrafts, Sericulture and Coir, Cardamom, Coffee etc. along with a special organisation for the development of modern small industry. All these Boards, except the last one were part of the Cottage Industry Board established in 1947.

The Industrial Policy Resolution of 1956 also highlighted the role of this sector in providing immediate large scale employment. The growth of small scale industries was considered all the more important in reducing urban congestion, reducing inequitable distribution of income and in the effective utilisation of local resources. The Industrial Policy Resolution of 1956 declared a policy of "supporting cottage and village and small scale industries by restricting the volume of production in the large scale sector". The Policy Resolution further stated that:

> *"While such measures continue to be taken, whenever necessary, the aim should be to ensure that the decentralised sector acquires sufficient vitality to be self supporting and that development is integrated with that of large industry. The State will therefore concentrate on measures designed to improve the competitive strength of small scale producers. For this it is essential that the technique of production should be constantly improved and modernised, the pace of transformation being regulated so as to avoid, as far as possible technological unemployment".*

Accordingly, a committee was appointed under the chairmanship of D.G. Karve to suggest measures to equip the sector to undertake the responsibilities assigned in the plan[9]. The main task of the Karve Committee was to recommend the measures to equip this sector in the following way:

1. The bulk of the increased production during the Plan period of consumer goods in common demand has to be provided by the village and small scale industries.
2. The employment provided by these industries should progressively increase; and
3. The production and marketing in these industries is organised, in the main, on co-operative lines.

The Committee recommended giving importance to research, and training, in village industries, handicrafts, and small scale industries. The Committee also suggested improvement in tools and equipments, expansion in training where the possibility of employment generation is clear etc.

The Mahalanobis model which formed the basis of India's early five-year plans, had assigned a well defined role to the small scale and rural industries[10]. This is often forgotten, Mahalanobis who looked at the issue in the context of overall development strategy, saw important role for small industry in meeting the growing demand for essential consumer goods. This can take place at a relatively low investment cost. In this process, this further creates, a significantly larger increase in employment than that would be generated by taking recourse to large scale factory production. Many programmes for promoting these industries have also been implemented. The main objective here is to build an industrial decentralised economy with an industrial structure like a programmed pyramid whose base would be a progressive rural economy and the growth of small industries units coupled with necessary services among the big villages and small towns all over the country" (Karve Committee Reporting). Out of the total protective measure taken for this purpose, 60 to 70 per cent of benefits went to the traditional industries (Vaidyanathan, 1991).

This role of small scale units was not exclusively confined to rural industries. Strictly speaking, till 1960 no policy measure was specifically taken to promote rural industrialisation. By the end of the Second Five Year Plan it was clear that not only had small units not developed appreciably outside the large urban centres, but also that there appeared to have been no substantial Government support to encourage such dispersal (Tyabji, P.144). To correct this, the Planning Commission constituted a Rural Industries Planning Committee in 1961 which in turn initiated a project for the development of small units in backward areas.

At the official level, the Third Plan Working Group on small scale industries suggested the use of industrial estates as a tool for regional industrial planning. As a result, during the Third Plan an extensive Rural Industrial Programme was implemented. The other objectives in this direction were the setting up of Industrial Development Areas in the backward regions, development of large projects as the nucleus of regional growth, planned development of village and small industries in the rural areas, small towns and less developed areas and preferential treatment to backward regions in training facilities and a programme for the development of human resources for the inaugural development of backward regions. But, all these programmes were implemented only to a limited extent (Vyasulu and Pandey, 1986; Vyasulu, 1987).

Thus, two committees, namely Pande Committee and Wanchoo Committee were appointed to look into the identification of backward areas and the other for fiscal and financial incentives to the sector[11]. After long deliberations on these recommendations the Government decided to give an investment subsidy of 10 per cent to the identified backward regions.

Thus, to achieve decentralised industrialisation, growth centres for rural industrialisation were adopted as part of the Backward Area Development Programmes in the Fourth Plan. These rural industrialisation programmes were spread extensively during the Fifth Plan period. But the programme had only a limited impact on the modernisation in rural areas. This is evident from several evaluation studies. For example, the study on Jaipur Industrial Estates (Kashyap, 1964), Industrial Estates in Gujarat (Desai and Kashyap, 1979; Kashyap, Shah and Pathak, 1976), and some other recent studies on Industrial Estates in Kerala, West Bengal and Mysore (cited by Sandesara, 1980) confirm this argument.

The Industrial Policy of 1977 (by the Janata Government) is noted for its thrust to the growth of village industries. The policy stated that:

> *"It is the policy of the government that whatever can by produced by small and village industries must only be so produced".*

Accordingly, reservation of production of the commodities, that can be produced in the small scale sector was increased from 180 items to more than 500 items. For the first time in industrial history, a "tiny sector" was defined as one with an investment in machinery and equipment up to Rs. one lakh and with location in towns with a population of less than 50,000. District Industries Centres were set up to promote the growth and spread of small scale industries. The main objective here was to improve the reach and effectiveness of the extension services. To discourage the growth of industries in the big cities and towns, regulations were put in place for issuing of new industrial licences in the specified areas.

The Industrial Policy Statement of 1980 gave prime importance to the correction of regional imbalances. For this a few nucleus plants in identified industrially backward districts were set up. It was expected that small industry will grow near the mother plant. Massive programmes were organised during the Sixth Plan to revitalise and develop existing traditional as well as modern industries. In order to achieve the objective of promoting growth of these industries, specific number of commodities were exclusively allotted for cottage industries. All the village and small industry development agencies were brought under the Industry Ministry. District Industrial Centres at the district level and Rural Marketing and Service Centres at the block level were established during this time. Central Government and some of the State Governments decided to purchase some of the articles needed by them from the village industries sector. The product reservation was increased from 180 to around 500 and now in 1994, it is around 800. But, most of these were beyond the production plan of the village sector, so it was produced by the urban small scale sector.

The Seventh Plan gave importance to the upgradation of technology and modernisation, mainly to improve product quality and to minimise costs. One of the distinguishable features is the support given to ancillarisation. The same thrust was given, to rural industrial development in the initial years of Eighth plan when the Janata Dal Government was in power. Soon after the announcement of the New Economic Policy in July, 1991, the Finance Minister announced the "Policy for Small, Tiny and Village Enterprises" in the Parliament on August, 8, 1991. The distinction of this policy from the earlier is on its shift from the basic frame work. Till then, all the industrial policies in India were within the policy frame of the Industrial Policy Resolution of 1956. The changes whatsoever made thereafter were all within the limit and access of this policy. The 1991 policy called for efforts to debureaucratise and deregulate the industrialisation process in India. The new policy substantially delicensed the industrial sector. The policy also recognised activities like service and business enterprises as part of tiny industries. Unlike the small scale sector, the tiny sector will be eligible for continuing support from the Government. How this works remains to be seen.

Incentives to Rural Industrialisation

The net result of the Government policies mentioned above were in the form of establishment of various institutions for the growth of the small scale sector. The policies in this direction from these organisations are in the form of either protection or promotion or both. The traditional and village industries enjoyed more protection and less promotion, whereas the opposite is true for the small scale sector. We will now mention these measures in brief separately for the modern and the traditional sectors.

The Modern Sector

Demarcation of the protective and promotional measures is on the basis of the investment limits. This limit is fixed by the Industrial Policy Resolutions of the Governments from time to time. An over view of the investment limits is shown in Table 2.1. This table shows that, the investment limit for the small scale sector has increased considerably over a time. The units within the

Table 2.1: Definitional Change of Small Enterprises

Change Over Time	*Investment Criterion*		*Employment Criterion*
	Normal SSU	*Ancillaries*	
Upto 1958	FC upto Rs.0.5 million	Same	Employment upto 50 workers if using power or upto 100 workers if not using power.
1959	The value of machinery was taken as the original price paid, irrespective of new or old machinery	-DO-	-DO-
1960	Gross value of fixed assets upto Rs. 0.5 million.	Gross value of fixed assets upto Rs.0.01 million.	Employment Criterion dropped.
Investment Limit Applicable only to Plan and Machinery Rs. Million			
1966	0.5	1.0	1 lakh
1975	1.0	1.5	Should be situated in towns with a population of less than 50,000
1977	2.0	2.5	
1980	3.5	4.5	For EOUs 2 lakh also
1985	6.0	7.5	Tiny enterprises includes SSU, service, business enterprises also.
1990			
1991			

EOU: Export Oriented Unit, SSU: Small Scale Units, FC: Fixed Capital

Source: Upto 1981, Tyabji, 1989, Upto 1985, Kashyap, 1988, upto 1997, NCAER.

investment limit can produce the products that come under the reserved list, enjoy a 10 per cent price preference for Government purchases and excise duty exemption/ concessions etc.

The table shows upward revision in the investment limit of the small scale sector. The employment criteria have been relaxed from time to time. From 1977 onwards tiny sector also came into the picture. The possible consequences of the upward revision of the investment limit need to be explained. An upward revision will always benefit the larger units in the small scale sector. The other possibility of it would be that very small units producing a similar item have to compete with the bigger units that enjoy these benefits. In fact, the investment limit itself is a disincentive to grow beyond the limit as the concessions are not allowed to bigger units. This may lead, not to growth, but to a multiplication of units, in which an entrepreneur may set up new small units rather than expand the existing one.

Policy Measures: Protection and Promotion

Different types of policy measures are classified into the policies of protection and promotion. This is summarised in Table 2.2.

Table 2.2: Policy Support to the Small Scale Sector

Protection	*Promotion*
1. Product Reservation	1. Provisions of infrastructure
2. Excise Exemption and Concessions	*(a)* Industrial Space
3. Government Purchase Programme	*(b)* Export Processing Zone
4. Capital Subsidy	*(c)* Industrial Parks
5. Import Tariffs	2. Sewage and waste Disposal
	3. Financial Assistance
	4. Technical and extension Service
	(a) Consultancy Services
	(b) Entrepreneurial Training

Source: Planning Commission Ninth Five Year Plan 1997-2000.

Protection

One of the striking protective policies is the product reservation. The product reservation, which started as a part of the "Common Production Programme" comprises two elements. The first is the reservation of the sectors of production to the small scale industries and secondly, not to allow the large scale sector to expand production in the sectors reserved for small scale units. But later, the idea of common production programme was totally forgotten, and the argument was for complete protection to the small scale sector. For example, under the 1978 Industrial Policy the statement was that, "whatever can be produced by small scale sector can be so produced"[12].

The result of neglecting the common production programme was the appearance of products of both the sectors in the market. This resulted in the poor allocative efficiency, poor quality and high prices in the economy. Sandesara 1993 points out that reservation has neither explicitly enhanced the growth of the firms nor has made any worthwhile contribution to productivity employing the abundant labour force by any clear cut standard empiricism (also see National Council for Applied Economic Research 1997). The point of allocative efficiency is all the more relevant in a developing country like India. The studies in the direction of efficiency differ from sector to sector, no conclusive evidence is obtained. In general there is a view that small scale industry is a better utiliser of labour not capital".

Another form of protective measure is excise exemption and concessions. The excise duty exemption now is up to 30 Lakhs of the ex-factory values. Excise exemptions and subsidy to the small scale sector cause a loss of more than 50 per cent of its excise revenue to the Government (NCAER, 1997). These types of concessions have their own advantages and disadvantages. Of course, this will give a competitive edge to the small firms in the markets. At the same time it may force the small firms to keep the output even at a low level; thus, it may not promote industrial growth. However, there is a hard evidence to assume that the slow growth of the middle sector is due to this type of protective policies.

Another form of protective measure is in the form of Government purchases[13] started from the Second Plan onwards. The Government purchases are in the form of preferred purchases, price preference and fiscal and procedural incentives. The main objective of the government purchase programme is to provide a larger market to the commodities produced by this sector.

Finally different types of concessions and subsidies are also a part of protection. There is the capital subsidy at the time of starting and after that concessions flow in the form of sales tax exemption, power subsidy, power exemption etc. Though, the possibility of misutilisation is high in all the protective measures, one policy that is to be highly objectionable is capital subsidy. It may work against intensive technology that is being adopted. This may force at least certain entrepreneurs to start the activity just to take advantage of the benefits. Thus, capital subsidy in general may not give the desired results. Till recently, import tariff was one of the foremost protective measure adopted by the Government to protect the Indian Industrial Sector from outside competition.

Promotion

As shown in the table, the promotional measures range from the provision of infrastructural facilities to the technical and extension services. All these promotional measures helped the growth of the small scale sector in India. One of the main elements of the promotional measures is the provision of infrastructure facilities to the industries. In this context, the role of the public sector was crucial and its role in the over all industrialisation is undoubtedly clear. The public sector alone is responsible for the huge infrastructure facilities conducive to the growth of the industrial sector in India.

The infrastructural facilities include the development of industrial space. Export Processing Zones, Growth Centres, Industrial Parks etc. Facilities for getting raw materials, power, and communications etc. were provided in these centres. For the purpose of sewage disposal, the Government has initiated a programme of Common Effluent Treatment Plant. To help the industries in their credit needs, SIDBI (Small Industrial Development Bank of India) is providing financial assistance through its various affiliates. The other institutions working in this field are National Small Industries Corporation, State Financial Corporations, Small Industries Investment and Development Corporations at the State level etc. During this time a huge bureaucracy was set up. Technical and other extension services consist of a variety of activities like provision of technical assistance and guidance, conducting of techno-economic surveys; provision of common facility workshops, tool room and testing facilities; conducting training programmes; preparing project reports, promoting ancillary and subcontracting relationships, assistance from District Industrial Centres etc.

The Effect of Government Policies

What is the result of all these programmes? This again depends on the way we look at the industrial development in India. Have the policies led the industrial structure in country into the healthy directions. The general pattern of growth observed from the experience of developed countries is in the form of a slow shift away from the small scale industrial production to the medium and large scale sector. But the result seems to be different in India. The particular situation that emerges in India is that it has not followed this pattern. There has been a decline in the growth of the traditional industries over the years, while the role of the small scale industries and large scale industries has increased considerably. The policy seems to have provided lesser help of this type to the medium scale sector (Little et al, 1987; NCAER 1997) as well as to the village industries. This also indicated the absence of shifting away from the small scale to the medium scale industries. The reason for this is a matter of detailed discussion. When we look into the over all industrialisation pattern over the plan period, considerable progress has been made. Sandesara (1992) found that:

> *"the general policy to subserve the objective of rapid industrial growth with special emphasis on the production of basic and heavy industries and on their production in the public sector seems to have its goal achieved."*

This is what the Bombay Plan of 1944 wanted.

Coming to the small decentralised sector, it was expected to promote decentralised development, as well as to promote balanced growth of the economy by reducing concentration of economic power (as mentioned in the Industrial Policy Resolution of 1956). This is again clear from the following findings of Sandesara. "But it is during the late sixties, that some serious thought on the dispersal of industrial activity among the different regions and the prevention of concentration of economic power in private hands is given. Thus, the objectives of increasing the industrial growth, reducing the concentration of economic power, regional balance were seen to be satisfactory (Sandesara, 1992, p. 112). This is again specific to the bigger units, as MRTP (Monopolies Restrictive Trade Practices Act, 1969) limit is one of the instrument of this erection.

When we look from the point of view of reducing regional disparities, and balanced growth of the small scale sector, there are diverging views. The Census Survey (1987-88) results show that dispersal of units has taken place in the country over a time (Sandesara, 1993). But the latest study conducted by the National Council for Applied Economic Research (1997) in this direction stated that, some dispersal and decentralisation of SSI growth has taken place. It does not seem to have been to the extent indicated by the second SSI Census. In general, small industries have tended to concentrate in the vicinity of large industries or in metropolitan and big cities.

There is reason to come to this kind of conclusion as, most of the units which come under Annual Survey of industries have an urban bias.

The NCAER (1997) study also brings into light other effects of the Government policies on this sector. Though the measures mentioned above attempted to promote the industrial growth in India, it also led to some kind of undesirable effects. The result was the absence of product quality improvement and interest in the expansion of exports. It does not mean that the existing share of the Small Scale Sector in exports is not satisfactory. All that may be said is that the high tariff barrier has created a kind of less serious attitude towards product quality improvement, which might be the result of the absence of external competition. When the Government control is exercised in the form of import licensing and tariff barriers, it may even create a kind of rent seeking activity in the economy (Santhonam Committee 1964)[14].

Another convergence is that the major beneficiaries of all these protective and promotional measures are the bigger units. Tiny units make little use of the promotional and extension services of subsidies, concessions etc. In general the tiny units were not the beneficiaries of Government support. The tiny units are in dire need of modernisation, technical guidance, credit, information/technological management and marketing assistance. The most surprising fact is that most of the units are not even aware of the existence of different types of incentives and concessions. This is also evident from the NCAER Survey of 657 small scale units in the country. The study reveals that among the 53 units producing reserved items, 19 units are not even aware that they are producing reserved items.

Another major element totally missing in the whole policy of the Government is the investment on Research and

Development. While there has been some talk of this in the KVIC sector, funds were not allotted for it. The Research and Development helps to improve the product quality, it increases the competitive strength of the industries and at the same time it also helps to find out cost effective methods of production. In view of the recent liberalisation, the proper Research and Development is the only factor that is capable of helping the small scale sector to compete with the foreign firms.

One very important factor that has come up simultaneously with the protective as well as promotion policies is the high bureaucratic control. The industrial sector both large and small, seemingly is, shackled in the bureaucratic control from top to bottom. This seemingly might have stopped the prospective entrepreneur to come to the small scale sector of the country. After the massive liberalisation and deregulation, we exactly do not know, how far the industrial sector is debureaucratised in the course of liberalisation and how much of it applies to rural, small industry.

However, the modern small scale sector witnessed satisfactory growth[15]. Some limited efforts have also gone into encouraging small units as ancillaries to a large scale units, especially in the public sector. Again, ancillarisation has its own limitations, such as increased dependency, low wages, high uncertainty etc. Yet another factor that determines the growth of small industry is the creative measures taken by the State Government within the larger policy frame stipulated by the Central government. In this paper we have not attempted to study the promotional policies followed by the State Governments.

Traditional Units

The first section clearly brings out the underlying factors for the growth of two divergent types in small scale industrial pattern in India. The way these industries treated were also different. The traditional and village industries were to perform the broad function of employment and social welfare. While the modern small scale sector concentrated on productivity and efficiency. Similar to the modern sector, the village industries were also protected from the rest of the sectors. The difference in this respect was that the modern small scale sector was protected from the medium and large scale sector while the traditional sector was protected from the small scale sector. In general the promotional measures were largely in favour of the small scale sector.

The traditional sector, unlike the modern sector, possesses certain characteristics of its own. We have earlier mentioned that, the traditional industries are a part of village life. Traditional sector was also the time away from the modern productivity or efficiency criteria. People have depended on this sector for decades and are still depending on it as a part of their life. Local tradition is the factor that made them concentrate on these activities.

The next aspect and a very important one is that the rural and village industries sector stands at the bottom of the industrial hierarchy in India. One of the resultant effects of this is that any fluctuation in the agricultural sector either in its output or in employment generation may affect this sector. This is all the more evident from the residual sector hypothesis of Vaidyanathan (1986). The residual sector hypotheses states.

> *"If the absorptive capacity of agriculture and of urban areas is limited, the pressure of excess labour supply in rural areas will fall more heavily on rural non agricultural sector, which means that the level of the rural non agricultural wage rate relative to the agricultural wage should be quite sensitive to the extent of imbalance between labour supply and demand in the rural areas" (Vaidyanathan, 1986 p A 1 & 2).*

The main reason for such a diversification is the distress of agricultural workers. Thus rural Industries are considered a "Strange Sector". This shows that agricultural labourers find it an alternative source of employment in their distress. In view of the high labour pressure in the agricultural sector, policies have to be evolved to pull labourers in to the rural industries. One of the ways to attract them would be comparatively high wages. In the present circumstances one cannot assure that, the industries like KVIC are providing comparatively better wages. This argument can be characterised by the high share of part time and casual workers in the KVI sector. The absence of any other better alternatives push the workers into these activities. Thus, KVI sector acts as a sponge sector.

Though the traditional industries include a variety of activities like Khadi and Village Industries, Coir, Handloom, Sericulture, Handicrafts, the largest industry is the KVI. The Khadi and Village Industries include activities like Khadi cloth production, manufacture of soaps, processing of agricultural commodities, blacksmithy, oil making. The planning process in India has been successful in formulating strong institutional agencies like KVIC for the growth of these activities.

The performance of these industries is not at all satisfactory. This can be understood from the dismal performances of KVI sector. As Jain puts it, "Though the Government policy in some measure has throughout been one of encouraging cottage and village Industries such encouragement till now has been largely symbolic. One reason is that these industries are truly not recognised as the most vital avenue next to agriculture for providing employment and income to the millions of unemployed and destitute[16] (Jain, 1980, P 1748). This is also true for the other traditional industries. The net result was that employment in traditional industries had in fact declined (Vaidyanathan, 1991).

This does not mean that the Government policies have totally failed in this direction. There are micro level studies to show that the policies of the State as well as Central

Government have helped the growth of the rural industries. For instance, D.B. Gupta (1982) in his study of rural industry in the Punjab region concludes that policies and programmes of the Government of India and the efforts of State Governments of Punjab and Haryana facilitated the development of rural industrial sector in these states. But this kind of instances are rare.

The problems of the traditional and village industries are wide ranging. They start from the Government policies and come down to the firm level. As mentioned above there is a decline of the Gandhian concept of self sufficient village economy. This is a fact revealed from the plan allocation to this sector[17]. As mentioned in the review of policies, though the Karve committee argues for upgradation for technologies and training to the workers to equip the sector to meet the consumer needs, most of the programmes in this direction are neither organised nor implemented. It is true that the KVIC has a programme of technology improvement and training etc. (see D.B. Gupta, 1993). But it does not seem to have had any impact. (See also Panditrao's paper in Bhalla and Reddy, 1994).

When we compare the nature of products being marketed by the KVIC, we can easily see the absence of diversification of this sector. Most of the products are expensive, inferior in quality and not very suitable to the changing consumer tastes. It is difficult to assume that, a traditional potter can survive in the advent of cheap and durable plastic and aluminium utensils. The marketing strategy of KVIC itself is sales led marketing. The Government rebates exist throughout the year for these products, and they are very complex and typical of the bureaucracy that runs this sector. An important reason for this can be attributed to the inferior technology used by this sector.

The Khadi and Village Industries Commission provides grant and loans to its various implementing agencies to get

KVI activated. Grants are generally for training, research and developmental activities, while loan is for production purposes including use as working capital. Out study of KVIC sector shows decelerating growth of grants to its implementing agencies. The implication of this trend is far reaching. One can easily assume that, it reduce the investment on research and developmental activities and thereby makes it less competitive in the changing conditions. In the present analysis it is observed that the earnings of the KVI are very low and they have also showed a declining trend. This reflects in the poor earnings of the workers, and this in turn could be due to poor productivity. It leads to a vicious circle.

One can, therefore, infer that, overprotection of these industries on ideological grounds in fact prevented the growth of traditional and village industries capacity to grow by facing the challenges from the market. In that case, the most important question from the policy point of view will be that in which framework and in what way can these industries be treated.

Along with the above policy questions, there are questions related to efficiency, employment, technology and productivity. The question of efficiency is largely related to the efficient utilisation of resources. There is a general belief that, small scale units are inefficient and cannot effectively utilise the capital. Their existence is mainly due to their suitability to the small villages and rural areas etc.

One of the factors that determines efficiency is technology improvement. We have the example of various units working on the traditional lines producing modern products, which have shown remarkable improvement in efficiency with proper technology adaptation. Some of these units have grown both vertically and horizontally. The workers who depend on these types of units are able to get good wages also. The firms of this nature are also able to produce high quality products comparable to modern enterprises. We do not have micro level information to show the level of technology, technology adaptation and workers' skill, environmental impact of these units. Thus, lessons are to be derived from these types of units to understand the factors leading to such a success. We also need to know much about the international experiences in this direction (Nanjundan, 1994).

One of the factors that emerge from the above review is that the traditional industries have been left far behind in over all industrial development. In the modern sectors the tiny sector in general was not able to enjoy the benefits of Government policies. This has certain effects on rural industrialisation. The tiny sector and a traditional village industries have become dispersed industries. This obviously shows the Government policy in this regard has not worked fruitfully. The fact that traditional and village industries, have not flourished implies that right kind of macro economic environment was not created and it is important to understand from this view point the inadequacies of the macro economic policies actually pursued. Another important point is the absence of attention to improve the overall training, research and developmental activities of the sector. Moreover in the light of significant reforms of macroeconomic policies presently implemented in India, it needs to be asked if the macroeconomic environment for the development of small scale industries will ever improve as a result[18].

Though this paper gives in brief a macro picture of the Government policies towards rural industries comprehensive micro level information of these industries is still lacking. Attempts have to be made in this direction to know the technology and employment aspects, workers skills, the effect of Government policies, their capacity for surplus generation and the environmental impact of these industries. This kind of study, both for modern and traditional industries can bring out the problems bewildering the sector and its potentials for future growth.

Artisan Industries

One of the basic objectives of development planning in recent years is improvement of the levels of living of the weaker sections of the community. The artisans and craftsmen who constitute a significant portion of the weaker sections in the industrial population in rural and semi-urban areas have received due attention. As a matter of fact, the thrust of the new economic policy is promotion of cottage and handicraft industries as a means, among others, of generating fuller employment and higher incomes to the artisans. But what is forgotten in the meanwhile is the feasibility of expanding the decentralised sector to the extent it is envisaged. As it is, this sector is facing a series of constraints imposed by the non-availability of the required organisational and production skills, basic inputs like raw materials and capital equipment, and, what is more, the limited markets owing primarily to wrong consumer preferences and competition from the organised sector. Any plan of expanding the centralised sector should first be preceded by the evolution of a series of policy measures for cushioning the impact of these problems. A prerequisite for policy formulation is a clearer understanding of production, marketing and organisational problems of the decentralised sector in the context of the role ascribed to it now. But the inadequacy of complete and up-to-date data about the various aspects of this sector is a handicap for assessing the present position and future potential of these industries. It is to meet this requirement, as it were, the All India Handicrafts Board, New Delhi has commissioned a series of evaluation research studies on the handicrafts.

As some studies are proposed to be taken up by the various research organisations located in different parts of the country it is considered desirable to concentrate on those handicraft industries which are unique to Andhra Pradesh and which hence, have less chances of being studied by other research organisations. The industries which are peculiar to Andhra Pradesh are Wood, Stone and Ivory Carving,

Lacquereware and Wooden-Toys, and Metalware, Carpentry, Cobblery, Blacksmithy, Goldsmithy, Bamboo Basket Making. Within the framework of time and resources constraints it was considered feasible to cover only the artisans in the trades of carpentry, cobblery, bamboo basketing, blacksmithy and goldsmithy artisans which are concentrated in Kurnool District.

The artisans who are engaged in the production of goods could be either the producer artisans or the wage-labour artisans. While the later work either with a manufacturer or with a master craftsman for piece wages, the former are the own account workers who produce the wares with simple tools and sell them to the dealers in the local market.

The interest of the present study is basically in the artisans and their socio-economic conditions. An appropriate way of looking at the levels of living of these artisans is first to see how they have reacted to the economic stimuli of changes in prices and technology. The levels of living may be then considered the product of this reaction of the groups. However, it may be noteworthy that the nature of reaction of any class of workers and the consequent levels of income cannot be related not only to the individual characteristics of the workers but also to the overall economic structure and relations of the society and distribution of resources and power among different sections of the society. Therefore, in the present study, though the focus is on the artisans and the economics of their operations, it is also proposed to examine the operations of the institutions built around the artisans. We are particularly interested in the dealers, who buy artisan product and the agencies, which supply various inputs to the artisans. One need not over-emphasise the fact that the inter relationships between the artisans and the aforesaid institutions will affect the levels of living of the artisans. Hence the justification for considering artisans socio-economic conditions in the socio-institutional context.

Role of Artisans in Rural Development

The Rural Scene

There is massive poverty in rural areas due to unemployment and lack of income opportunities. The small land holdings of rural farmers are not adequate to support large families. As a result people from the rural areas migrate in large numbers to urban areas, and the exodus is ever on the increase. The recent trend of globalisation has exacerbated the problems of rural areas as the village industries are further marginalised. The global industries are entering into consumer sectors where Vllage and Khadi Industries were once popular. Further more, village industries are not able to compete with big industries in mass manufacturing and marketing. Thus the process of globalisation has accentuated the "rural drift".

The main strategy should therefore be to stop the migration of unskilled people from rural area to the town. Villagers who migrate to the cities face worse situation not being able to earn a decent income. In villages, they have their homes and the communities to work with. In the cities they live in filth and squalor. This trend to overcrowd the existing cities create enormous problems for development. Attempts should be made to halt this alarming process by enabling people to generate income opportunities in villages. This should be done through optimum utilisation of both human and physical resources available in villages, through revitalising village industries which are dying due to lack of updated skill and knowledge. Although there is a national realisation of Gandhian approach that India will not prosper until the villages are made economically viable, there are no proven models of doing so. The challenge is to break new ground with a unique approach to rural development, which may include designing and disseminating new technology for income generation.

Over the years, the Governments of developing countries have adopted positive measures to defeat the forces of stagnation. To perform this gigantic task a well considered and suited policy of economic development has been framed. The growth process of these countries aims at accelerating economic development to enhance social welfare. In fact, the economic change is a part of a wider social change and the economic development is a long-term process of intrinsic growth. Therefore, the task of policy making has a vital role to play in selecting the desired objectives and suitable alternatives for stimulating the economic growth. It also requires a careful examination of the existing institutional framework, social values, economic requirements and their implications, keeping in view the need for rapid social and economic development of the economy.

India has a long and rich tradition of traditional village industries. In pre-British period Indian handicrafts were famous and had a world-wide reputation. However, the Village Industries, to a greater extent were destroyed as a result of step-motherly policy of British rule in India.

In modern India the importance of cottage and village industries is manifold. After agriculture, village industries are regarded as the second important source of livelihood of rural people. The traditional industries provide employment opportunities not only to one generation but to several generations. Owing to high employment potential and low capital output ratio, traditional and village industries have a vital and significant role to play in India. Massive rural industrialisation programmes are called for to reduce the incidence of unemployment and under-employment, to increase national income, to accelerate economic growth by making an optimum use of available resources, to promote balanced regional development, to reduce inequalities in the distribution of income and wealth, to reduce the present excessive pressure on land and overcrowding in urban areas, and to promote the exports.

In the post Independence era an impressive growth of village industries in terms of size, employment generation, net domestic product, exports earning etc., has been recorded. The development of cottage Industries is an integral part of the overall economic, social and industrial development of the country. Keeping in view the importance of these Industries Government of India paid special attention in planning for economic development. In order to promote the growth of village industries, a variety of supportive measures have been adopted by the Government. Some of the important measures are; reservation of certain goods for exclusive production in the Village and Cottage Industries, provision of adequate financial support, provision of various measures for export assistance, for export promotion, provision of training of management skills to the entrepreneurs and establishment of regional information centres.

Rural Artisan Programmes

The village community traditionally, is an entity based on family groups. These groups have certain autonomy. The group of artisans used to assume a separate entity in the village life[19]. Artisans traditionally belonged to the professions of blacksmith, carpentry, pottery, cobblery, goldsmithy, weaving and oil extraction. They used to provide effective support and servicing facilities for the economic activities, making and repairing household tools and farm equipment in the village. In return they used to get a fixed share of the peasant's produce and raw material for producing the equipments and household tools[20]. Godgil while describing this close unity, viewed agriculture and artisan sectors as indistinguishable and termed artisan as village servants, who were to serve the needs of the peasants and villagers and therefore, played a subordinate role in the village economy[21].

The Rural Artisan Programme is a part of the Small Farmers Development Agency (SFDA), Marginal Farmers and Agricultural Labourers (MFAL), launched by the Ministry of Agriculture as a Central scheme in 87 selected areas all over the country in 1971-72. This programme aims at upgrading the skill of identified rural artisans by way of providing training in the use of improved tools and equipments to meet the changing need of the rural economy. Again the main purpose is to develop self-employment opportunities and to help increase the earnings of the weaker sections of the community. The artisans in the rural areas, despite their rich heritage and skills, belong to the poverty group. A programme aimed at upgrading their skills and supplying them with modern toolkits has been in operation since 1992. So far about two lakh artisans have been assisted with improved toolkits. The scheme with focus on handicrafts artisans, leather workers, wood and stone workers, metal workers like blacksmiths, goldsmiths has been extended to the entire country. The TRYSEM programme has recently been modified to import modern skill training to all categories of artisans and to supply them with improved or power driven toolkits. The programme aims at checking unemployment among the artisans and stopping their migration to urban centres by improving their production capabilities and consequently their productivity and income.

Rural Industries Project

The Planning Commission sponsored the Rural Industries Programme (RIP) as a centrally sponsored scheme initially in 49 districts in 1962-63 with the basic objective of "expeditious growth of village industries and creation of opportunities for fuller and additional productive employment in rural areas[22]. Formerly the duration of the programme was 11 years, but later on, observing its effectiveness in increasing the industrial production and enlarging the employment opportunities, the period was extended further to twenty years to cover the entire country. The area of operation is the entire district, leaving, apart towns having a population of about 15,000. Five new projects were also taken up in 1971. In the Fifth Plan 57 new projects were further added particularly in industrially backward districts.

Under the scheme the Central Government provides financial assistance by way of grants towards the entire cost of establishment of the project organisation. The grants are also given for promotion of schemes like training programmes and common facility services. The project thus set up, renders the following kinds of assistance to rural artisan units.

1. Technical guidance before and after starting a unit.
2. Preparation of feasibility reports.
3. Making arrangements for loan facilities from commercial banks on easy terms.
4. Making arrangements for hire-purchase of machinery, marketing, raw materials and for marketing.
5. Providing in-plant training facilities, common facilities service, etc.

According to the data available, about 30,650 units have come up under this project, generating employment for about 82,000 persons. The gross value of production comes to Rs. 3.5 Crores.

The Rural Industries Project has revealed ample capacity to create job opportunities. During the period from 1984-85 to 1996-97, Jobs for 60,000 persons were created. The Institute of Manpower Research while examining the impact of Rural Industries Project made the following observations.

1. Analysis based on the sampled Artisans reveals that the rural artisans, by and large have not been able to avail themselves of the new opportunities introduced by recent rural development activities. The existing training facilities take a long time for acquisition and the practising artisans are not in a position to be away from their work for a long period.
2. The Special Programmes for the training of rural artisans being organised by the Rural Industrial Projects have not proved very useful, as the structure

of the courses is not in conformity with the requirements of the rural areas.

However the Rural Industrial Projects has made some dent on the development of rural industries, if not on the rural economy as a whole. A number of commercial banks and the State Governments have evinced keen interest in providing necessary financial, technical as well as infrastructural assistance. When the Rural Industrial Projects is transferred to the Small Industries Development Organisation a number of measures will be taken for speedy growth of these artisan units.

Need of Artisans

The needs of rural artisans and other small industries have received much attention from the planners and other agencies involved in rural development, who have realised the significance of rural development for alleviating the rural economy. Firstly, at present a large segment of rural population continues to depend on agriculture and other allied activities for their subsistence. The industrial sector is unable to absorb the growing population, and the agriculture sector is already burdened with the growing unemployment and underemployment. It is in this context, that it would be necessary for us to revitalise the traditional village and cottage industries involving the artisans. This is one way through which we can bring about some degree of rural upliftment and can lift artisans out of the poverty trap. There is a growing realisation for harmonious growth of the economy. There is need for encouraging and promoting rural artisans.

Secondly, there is a need for protecting human skills. The rural artisans are labour intensive and as such they can create more employment. It is observed that "The Employment Potential of this sector is four times more than that of large scale units". Hence to create greater employment potential the artisan industry has to be developed.

Thirdly, in a future strategy of economic development, secondary activity has necessarily to be started close to the primary sector, especially when the raw material is available. The rural population of India possesses latent resources and talents. These may be exploited fully for the benefit of the rural artisans.

Fourthly, the family as an economic unit of operation can be viable as an efficient household industry, where all the members of the family work under a common roof irrespective of differences of sex, age and work time etc. Any instrument or a piece of equipment which can be operated by all members of the family may be less productive strictly when operated personwise, but can be, with effective supervision, highly productive machine wise and in the ultimate cost-benefit analysis. This pattern of production could be more productive.

Fifthly, the high rate of population growth in India is the result of decline in death rate and increase in birth rate, and the population increased to 100 crores in 2001. The population growth does not hinder the country as long as it has abundant natural, financial and technological resources. It is not however advisable to allow population growth beyond these available resources. Then the government has to take measure to control population on one hand, and on the other to provide basic facilities to make people happy. One of such important facilities is government's provision of some training to rural youth. The main aim of the training is to equip the rural youth with necessary skill and technical knowledge to enable them to take up self-employment in different vocations. But if we observe carefully no country in the world is free from the fear of unemployment problem and our country is no exception. The country is very much confronted with the unemployment problem. But only the Government is capable to solve this problem, because no private agency can do it immediately and perfectly. Hence we need Governments action to solve this social problem.

Development Issues of Artisans

According to the National Productivity Council, an artisan is a self account worker or a wage earner engaged in the manufacture of tangible products largely through the application of his skills which are acquired either traditionally or through formal training and which are not personalised services of any nature[23]. In many parts of the country the artisans are a socially and economically depressed lot. They do not belong to the ownership class to supplement their income from agriculture. The economic status of traditional artisans performing activities like weaving, carpentry, blacksmithy, wood and ivory carving, masonry, cobbling, pottery etc. is determined by the scale of earnings from work participation, the size of Industrial and household assets by the level of technology assimilation and by the magnitude and effectiveness of official development initiatives etc. Educational backwardness, poor industrial and household asset base, competition from the factory system etc. have precipitated instability in their employment and earnings over a period. Marginalisation of those classes from the main stream economic activity and the large scale eviction/displacement of the most artisans from traditional occupations have exposed them to the risks of falling incomes, unstable employment and poverty.

They being scattered mostly in rural areas, the artisans have not been able to organise themselves into effective groups. Their levels of skills are generally low and they use tools and equipment which are outmoded and of low productivity. These artisans are observed to work as Individuals with some of the family members, mainly sons who assist them as and when the need arises[24].

Rural artisans face difficult market conditions. The declining demand for some of the traditional items produced by the artisans and their limited diversification into production of new items have contributed to this phenomenon[25]. In terms of assets, the artisan households were found to rank just above the agricultural labour households in the village society. In terms of their activity status, no perceptible change from traditional status is evident as most of them remain self employed. Some artisans however also market conditions. Some micro studies show that while individuals from non-artisan castes have entered the artisan activities, some traditional artisans have shifted to other occupations[26].

The impact of modernisation has by and large failed to percolate down to a prominent segment of the rural economy, the unorganised sector of artisans[27].

Moreover, no permanent linkages are established between the taker of the technology and its developer once the technology is handed over to the user. As a result, today most of the artisans are struggling for survival on their skills, evolved over thousands of years and now getting dissipated and blunted[28]. Their progeny is neither willing, nor able to carry on the family tradition and thus a rich culture is on the verge of extinction[29]. There is ample scope for improving the traditional skills of artisans through the application of modern technology. Given the woeful gaps in the organisation and leadership of the village artisans, their development and welfare depend mainly on the extent and effectiveness of State initiative.

State initiative towards empowerment of artisans in Andhra Pradesh consists of (1) Certain Welfare Schemes and (2) Development Corporations and schemes established for promotion of their employment, productivity and earnings, the Andhra Pradesh Handloom Workers Welfare Fund Scheme, the A.P. Khadi and Village Industries Commission, and the Special Programme for the Supply of Tool kits to Rural Artisans. The District Rural Development Agency is giving subsidies to the artisans under IRDP Programme and also arranging training to artisans in need of it. The APSFC and Commercial Banks are assisting artisans by providing Finance for setting up Artisan Complexes.

Role of Artisans Sector in Industrialisation of India

India is often described as an underdeveloped country. The term underdeveloped implies that the resources such as human and material of the country have not been properly harnessed, with the result that the people live in poverty. They are underfed and physically weak and their working capacity is low. Underdevelopment implies that the level of real income and capital per head of population is low as Judged by the standards in developed countries of North America and Western Europe. In underdeveloped countries, there is no large-scale application of the fruits of scientific and technological advances to agriculture and industry. Subsistence production is generally important for the people, the markets are comparatively narrow and manufacturing industry is usually unimportant[30].

In many developing countries, manpower is relatively abundant. It is therefore, imperative that their full and effective utilisation should become a focal point of socio-economic policies. Emphasis should be laid on small scale industries to absorb the surplus manpower in these countries.

Even after the emergence and rapid growth of the modern large scale industries, the small traditional and decentralised industries continue to play very important role in the economy. While one reason for the survival and importance of this sector lies in the fact that the large scale modern industry has not been able to absorb workers to the extent of effecting a shift from the traditional and small sector, and another more important reason for this phenomenon lies in the emphasis laid on the co-existence of different sectors and promotion of small and village industries in the industrial policy followed in the post independent India.

The village and small industries sector consists broadly of (1) modern small scale industries including tiny units and power looms and (ii) Traditional Industries namely handlooms, Khadi and Village industries, sericulture, handicrafts and coir industry. While the modern small scale industries and power loom use mostly power operated appliances and machinery with some technology sophistication and are generally located close to or in the urban areas including the large industrial centres, the traditional industries are generally artisan based and are located mostly in rural and semi-urban areas and involve lower levels of investment in machinery and provide largely part-time employment.

Artisan units use locally available raw materials, work on them with simple tools and sell their products in a local market. The artisan sector is unable to influence the creation of necessary infrastructure for its efficient functioning, and has to depend upon already available infrastructure.

The Industrial Policy Resolution of 1956 states that, while the policy of supporting cottage and village industries by restricting the volume of production in the large scale sector, by differential taxation or by direct subsidies is continued, the aim of the state policy will be to ensure that the decentralised sector acquires sufficient vitality to be self supporting and its development is integrated with that of large scale industry.

Artisan sector play an important role in the pattern of industrial development. The development of artisan industries is a means of promoting a large scale employment and also a means of meeting the increasing demand for consumer goods. The Industry Policy Statement of 1980, state that "The Government is determined to promote such a form of Industrialisation in the country that can generate economic viability in the villages. Promotion of suitable industries in rural areas will accelerate the generation of higher employment and higher per capita income for the villages in the country without disturbing the ecological balance. Handlooms, handicrafts, khadi and other village industries will receive greater attention to achieve a faster rate of growth in the villages." With a view to promoting artisan industries, the Government of India has set up organisations like Khadi and Village Industries Commission, All India Handlooms and Handicrafts Boards, Central Silk Board, Coir Board, All India Powerloom board, Development Commission for Small Scale Industries, Handlooms and Handicrafts, District Rural Development Agency etc. The Government has also taken measures to provide subsidies and concessional finance supply for the purchase of tool kits. It has also set up common facility centres like tool rooms, testing centres etc. It has constructed common work sheds. The future strategy in the case of traditional artisan industries should be to raise the productivity and income levels of artisans engaged in these industries rather than get more people employed. New work opportunities have to be generated in village industries. This will require a massive effort at skill formation and technological upgradation in artisan households in rural areas and small towns.

Rural artisans have played a very significant role in the productive activity of the village. Since the ancient times, while agriculture has been the main stay of the village economy, the artisans have fulfilled most of the day-to-day needs of the people. They have subserved the needs of agricultural sector by producing and repairing agricultural implements agricultural produce has been converted by them into usable commodities like cloth, oil etc., for local use as well as for supply to the urban areas. The contribution of the artisans in maintaining a self-reliant economy of the village is thus very significant[31].

Artisans constitute a sizeable segment of the work force. They have inherited the skills and have the potential to develop further. The dexterity with which they carry out their work is praiseworthy as well as amazing. Their products meet not only the demands in the domestic market of a village or group of villages. They have found markets in foreign countries too[32]. Traditionally, village artisans supply products and maintenance service to agricultural farmers in the village. They also produce goods to meet local demands. This category would usually cover carpenters, cobblers, rope-makers, blacksmiths, goldsmiths, potters, cloth and mat weavers etc.

Rural artisans play a very important role in the Indian economy. They are mostly self-employed. The objective of poverty eradication can be achieved only through providing employment opportunities to the growing labour force. By promoting self-employment one can hope to provide the growing labour force with opportunities for earning decent incomes. These artisans also contribute a substantial portion to the income generated in the country[33].

Till the advent of mechanised industry, artisan crafts met the entire needs of rural life and occupations in respect of tools equipment, furniture and other facilities. Even now artisans crafts continue to meet to some extent the needs of the weaker sections of the population. Further artisan skills are mostly inherited and very little expenditure or effort is devoted to their development.

New technological inventions led to increasing mechanisation of productive-activity; production started getting centralised in urban areas; more and more sophisticated machinery was increasingly being used for mass production of goods for large markets. This also resulted in the migration of impoverished artisans from rural to urban areas in search of livelihood. The number of village artisans who formed 18 per cent of the rural population in 1901 declined to 7 per cent by 1971[34].

In spite of technological inventions and developments, rural artisans play a very significant role in the Indian economy. They are the pillars of rural society. The artisans have played an important role in the development of native technologies. They have the ability to do the required job, provided sufficient encouragement is given to them.

Conditions of Rural Artisans

In terms of economic and social status, the artisans are no better than agricultural labourers. Rural artisans belong to the poorer sections of the rural population. Nearly 75 per cent of the artisans fall in the category of weaker sections of the rural families with their assets remaining below Rs. 3,500 in 2001.

Artisans constitute an important segment of the rural community. In 1991-census out of the total households, 29 Lakh (2.4 per cent of the total) were rural artisan households. There were about 1.5 million rural artisans engaged in various industries according to the 2001 census.

The rural artisan is a skilled worker in a traditional village craft. He works on his own. The rural artisans mostly utilise locally available resources for manufacturing, processing and servicing of a product or an activity. They are engaged in procuring a wide variety of products like carpets, brassware, earthenware, textiles and artistic pieces for the local people. They also supply a wide variety of implements to agriculturists.

The rural artisans who lack the new skills are made to abandon their traditional occupations. The artisans could not be integrated with the process of modernisation of agriculture. As a result of intensification of rural industrialisation programme and modernisation of the farm sector, the demand for artisans has been gradually increasing. But, unless they upgrade their skills to a large extent in tune with new developments in the rural sector, they cannot hope to get gainful employment. The formal training to rural artisans is imparted through specific training institutions like District Industries Centres, Industrial Training Institutes and Khadi and Village Industries Commission.

In almost all developmental programmes, the rural artisans were not given their due place. However, the artisan is an important person in the rural society because he contributes a lot to the development of techniques of making a bullock cart, a chaffcutter, plough, agricultural tools etc. The present technological development has broken the traditional linkages between the farmers and artisans. Hence there is a fall in the number of artisan households.

Plight of Rural Artisans

According to the All-India Debt and Investment Survey conducted during 1971-72, the rural artisan households formed just 2.4 per cent of the total number of rural households. They are among the poorest of the poor. Their holdings of assets were estimated at Rs.455 Crore, constituting a negligible proportion of 0.5 per cent of the total assets of rural households in 2001. The average holdings of the assets by the artisans was found to be Rs. 3,500 of which not more than eight per cent were in the form of implements and machinery, while the humble dwellings amounted to for as much as 57 per cent of the assets.

The average debt per household was Rs. 2000 out of which cash debt totalled to Rs.1800. Bulk of cash debt was due to non-institutional agencies (95 percent) among whom the most important ones were agricultural money lenders. The Government provided 2.7 per cent of the total, followed by co-operatives (1.7 percent) and commercial banks (0.3 percent). Of the total outstanding cash debts of Rs. 52.69 Crores of the artisan households on June 30, 2001, loans taken for production purposes were a marginal Rs. 12 Crore only.

Cash advances to artisans from commercial.banks stood at only Rs. 127.67 crore, in 6,27,120 borrower accounts at the end of June, 2001.

A study conducted in 2001 by the Madras Institute of Development Studies (MIDS) on rural artisans reveals that the new earnings per artisan per year worked out to be Rs. 1,081 in village leather, Rs. 1,816 in village pottery, Rs. 2,750 in carpentry and blacksmithy and Rs. 2,858 in bamboo activities..

No doubt, the importance of rural artisans has declined due to the emergence of industrial alternatives. But, it needs to be noted that artisans still play an important role in the growing industrialised economies. Given the socio-economic conditions in rural India, the rural artisans need to be projected and encouraged to expand their operations for maximum financial benefits.

With the modernisation of agriculture and small scale units, the demand for skilled manpower will substantially be increased. Then, the rural artisans can stay in their own villages and enhance their income with enough employment opportunities being available.

Trade Profile

Rural artisans constitute an important segment of the rural population. Artisans specialise mostly in traditional crafts which have their roots in the culture and life style of the communities handed down from generation to generation. Their work is characterised by a high standard of craftsmanship on par with the best in the world. If quality has suffered at times, it is on account of decline in demand and on account of the various problems faced by artisans. The problems have, to a large extent, remained unsolved. Consequently most rural artisan households as also other cottage industries are in the doldrums and are unable to provide a viable means of livelihood.

The study is mainly restricted to certain major categories of trades in Kurnool District. The Important rural

Table 2.3: Trades Selected for Survey in Kurnool District

Sl. No.	*Name of Trade*	*No. of Artisans*
1.	Carpentry	20
2.	Blacksmithy	20
3.	Cobblery	20
4.	Bamboo Basket Making	20
5.	Goldsmithy	20
	Total	100

household industries in the district are blacksmithy, carpentry, bamboo basket making, leather tanning, broom making pottery, stone carving, rope making, brick making, goldsmith, mat weaving, stone cutting and kalankari.

The villages and the rural artisan trades selected for survey in Kunool District are given in Table 2.3.

Carpentry: This has been a traditional trade in the villages although it has assumed a sophisticated function in the modern urban style of living. The village carpenter has inherited the trade and the skill from his predecessors in the family. He uses traditional tools and equipment to turn out form implements such as ploughs and carts and also household furniture and building materials. Almost all the agriculturist families engage him for some work or the other. In most cases, the wood is supplied to him by the customer, the carpenter gets his returns in the form of grain or as cash for work on contract. He is however, not engaged in this work throughout the year. Incidentally this is wholly a male occupation. About 2.137 artisans are reported to be engaged in this trade in the district with an investment of Rs. 3.8 Lakh in the shape of tools and equipment. It is rather difficult to single out places of concentration of carpentry as every village has a few carpenter families. Still from the data available, the trade is relatively more in Atmakur, Nandyal, Velugodu, and Sreesailam Revenue Mandals for the reason of wood being easily available from forests in these mandals.

Blacksmithy: The Blacksmith is another indispensable artisan in the village. Agricultural requisites of traditional type and to some extent hardware items such as door springs, hooks and door supporters are turned out by the blacksmiths. Again like carpentry it is a male occupation. Most of them like carpenters, work for the agriculturists from whom they receive fixed payment both in kind and cash. Their importance seems to have increased with the impact of fast agricultural development in some parts of the district. As per the data available there are around 1247 blacksmiths in the District, largely concentrated in Dhone, Yemmiganur, Nandyal, Adoni, C. Belagal Revenue Mandals. They use mostly traditional tools and equipments in which a sum of Rs. 2.14 Lakh is invested. It is difficult to estimate the consumption of raw materials, which are chiefly Iron and Wood, as the customers themselves supply them along with orders for finished implements.

Bamboo Basket Making: 2285 artisans are reported to be engaged in bamboo basket weaving. It is a seasonal activity. This Artisan group is reported to be largely found in Atmakur, Kothapalli, Velgode, Rudravaram, Gonegandla Revenue Mandals. Investment in this trade is very small. The tools and equipments in this trade are Knives, Wooden Softner, Files, Hand Saw etc. A good number of basket weavers are also reported to be engaged in making Jalla (a long basket wover of strips of bamboo to form the body of a cart) which is fixed on to carts for transport purposes. They also make straw roofs for huts in the villages. Economic returns are woefully low in this trade, which drives the artisans to take to other source of livelihood, particularly agricultural labour. The most downtrodden among these artisans lead a nomadic life, weaving mats, baskets and making broomsticks with orate leaves.

Among the trades bamboo work is confined to Atmakur and Srisailam Revenue Mandals, in which about 540 units are reported to be engaged. Presently the trade has declined with the advent of plastics and the families of this trade have taken to other occupations, mainly cultivation.

Cobblery: Kurnool district has a significant size of schedule caste population, chammaras for whom leatherwork has been a traditional caste occupation. There are 1771 cobblers in the district. The traditional articles turned out are tanned hides, desi chappals, water carriers and leather ornaments for the cattle. There is a considerable under employment among them. They are hardly engaged for about 150 days in a year. They are ordinarily poverty stricken and as artisans their method of production is crude and traditional. Most of the artisans, for want of employment have taken to other types of occupations, namely agricultural labour. In places very close to urban areas, the unemployed and under employed cobblers have taken to rickshaw pulling which fetches Rs. 25/- a working day on an average.

The tools and equipment commonly used in this trade are Knifes, hammer, cuttingplier, scissors, stitching, needles, punches, stone pieces, earthen pots or buckets and metal bases. Very few among Cobblers use sewing machines for stitching purposes. On an average Rs. 75/- is invested, in the trade by a cobbler family. Raw hides and skins are purchased locally or collected from surrounding areas Very crude methods are employed for tanning purposes. The tanned hides are mostly used by cobblers themselves in making chappals and other articles, the upper leather sheets etc. are procured from Hyderabad. Raw material and finance are the main problems of this trade at present.

Goldsmith: The goldsmith is also one of the indispensable artisan in the district. There are nearly 1218 goldsmith units in the district. Like carpentry, blacksmith trade too is a male occupation. Most of the goldsmiths are attached to the towns for reason of patronage. A goldsmith works on one of the few most precious metals with very few tools. A goldsmith has a very small crucibles in one of which he keeps gold mixed with a very small amount of copper and melts them together to give gold toughness and tempers the metal. Then with a small hammer and needle like tool, he moulds the metal in his hand into different ornaments and jewellery of artistic shapes, and sizes as required by his customers. He shows his entire workmanship in making ornaments. A perfect goldsmith can mould a single gram of gold into either a beautiful ring or an ear ring or a nose-stud. He executes his work more diligently and brilliantly as well. When the finished object is seen, one cannot but wonder at the workmanship and artistic talent of the goldsmith. The goldsmith gives different names to the ornaments he makes. He is a creator like a potter, who shapes a lump of mud into an urn, a goblet, a pitcher, a pot and a flower vase. Such is the workmanship of a goldsmith. It demands patience, observation, a keen eye for minute details and above all perfect imagination and an awareness of up-to-date changes in the Industry of ornament making.

REFERENCES

United Nations Organisation, "Report on the Process and Problems of Industrialisation in underdeveloped Countries", New York, United Nations, 1955, p. 16.

Gunnar Myrdal, "An International Economy", New York, Harpet & Brothers, 1956, p. 226.

Ibid., p. 226.

C. Ganguli, "Studies in Indian Economic Problems", Calcutta, 1978, p. 1.

National Institute of Small Industry Extension Training Industrial Policy Resolution, 1980, Hyderabad, NISTEL, 1980 p. 2.

Ibid., p.8.

Government of India, The First Five Year Plan—Draft outline (New Delhi Planning Commission, 1951), p. 162.

Government of India, Second Five Year Plan (New Delhi, Planning Commission, 1956), p. 429.

Government of India, Third Five Year Plan (New Delhi: Planning Commission, 1970), p. 284.

Government of India, Fourth Five Year Plan (New Delhi: Planning Commission, 1970), p. 284.

Government of India, Fifth Five Year Plan 1974 Volume II (New Delhi: Planning Commission, 1970), p. 160.

Government of India, Sixth Five Year Plan 1980-85 (New Delhi, Planning Commission, 1980) p. 186.

State Bank of India (1988), Seventh Five Year Plan (1985-90), Monthly Review June, p. 308.

Ibid. p. 309.

"Eight Plan Proposals" (1990) Economic Times Daily 31st December, pp. 1.

Government of India, Report of the Village and Small Scale Industries Committee, Second Five Year Plan, New Delhi, Planning Commission, October, 1955. p. 6.

Alexander, P.C. Industrial Estate in India", Bombay Asia Publishing House, 1963 p.

Government of India, Report of the working group on Identification of Backward Areas (Pande Working Group Report), Planning Commission.

Government of India, Report of working Group of Fiscal and Financial Incentives for starting industries in Backward Areas (Report of Wanchoo Working Group: Development Commissioner, SSI, Ministry of Industrial Development).

Ram, K. Vepa, Rural Industrial Development, Development Commissioner, SSI, New Delhi, p. 246.

Small, Industry – The Challenge of the Eighties, New Delhi, Vikas Publishing House Pvt. Ltd. 1983, p. 60.

Sutcliffee R.B. Industry and under Development Addisas Wesley Publishing Co. London (1971) p. 3.

Barn P.A., Political Economy of Growth, New York (1962), p. 277.

Colnean D and Ninon P.F. Economic of Changes in Less Developed Countries Philip Allan Publisher Ltd., Oxford (1978) p. 180.

UNIDO Industrial Development Strategy Reprinted in (Gerald M. Meier and edited) Leadiong issues in Economic Development (3rd edition) Oxford University Press, New York (1976), p. 180.

Rosenstein Radan P.N. Problems of Industrialisation of Eastern and South Eastern Europe, Economic Journal (June-Sept. 1943).

Third Five Year Plan—Summary Planning Commission, Government of India, p. 47.

Fourth Five Year Plan: 69-74, Planning Commission, Government of India, p. 399.

Sixth Five Year Plan 80-85 Planning Commission, Government of India, p. 86.

Ibid, p. 87.

Government of India, Report of the Working Group on the Identification of Backward Area, Planning Commission, New Delhi, 1965, Page, 5.

Government of India, Fiscal and Financial Incentives for Starting Industries in Backward Areas, Development Commissioner (S.S.I.), New Delhi, 1969 p. 2-3.

Government of India, Fiscal and Financial Incentives for Starting Industries in Backward Areas, Development Commissioner, (SSI), New Delhi, 1969, pp. 16-17.

Government of India, Report on Industrial Dispersal, National Committee on the Development of Backward Areas, Planning Commission, New Delhi, October, 1980, p.12.

See Appendix for six points Formula and Appendix–2 for the Taluqs Declined backward in Different Districts under Six Point Formula.

Government of A.P., Sixth Five Year Plan 1980-85, A.P., Department of Planning and Cooperation, Hyderabad-1980, p. 234.

Government of Andhra Pradesh, Report a Technical Committee on Identification of Backward Areas in Andhra Pradesh. Finance and Planning Department, Hyderabad 1981, pp. 2-6.

Chadha G.K. (1993): Policy support for Non-Farm Development in Rural India Some issues, National Seminar on Policy Environment for Rural Non-Farm Sector in India, Institute of Development Studies, Jaipur, September 10-11.

Chadha G.K. (1994): Industrialisation Strategy and the Growth of Rural Industry: The past experience, Draft paper presented in the workshop on Rural industrialisation in India, ILO-SAAT, New Delhi.

Gupta, D.B. (1982): Rural Industry in India—The experience of Punjab Region, Hindustan Publishing Corporation, New Delhi.

Government of India, (1985): The Seventh Five Year Plan, 1985-90, Vol. II, Planning Commission, October, 1985, pp. 99, 103.

Islam Riswanul (1987): Rural Industrialisation and Employment in Asia; ILO-RTEP, New Delhi, pp. 1-323.

Jain LC (1980); Development of Decentralised Industries: A review and some suggestions, Economic and Political Weekly, October, pp. 1747-1754.

Karve D.G. (1955) Village and Small Scale Industries (Second Five Year Plan) Committee 1956-Report, Manager Publications, New Delhi, pp. 1-85.

Kashyap S.P., P.G. Pathak and Jayasree Shah (1876): Industrial Estates in Gujarati: A preliminary study of linkage pattern, in P.N. Mathur (ed): Economic Analysis of Input-Output Framework, Vol. 3.

Kashyap S.P. (1964): Government sponsored industrial growth. The Jaipur Industrial Estate: A case study". The Economic Weekly, Vol. No. 16, pp. 1021-1027.

Kashyap S.P. (1988): Growth of Small Size enterprises in India: Its Nature and Content, World Development, Vol. No.16, No. 16, pp. 667-681.

Kashyap S.P. (1983): Emerging Tendencies in Rural Manufacturing Sector: Role of Policy, paper presented in the National Seminar on Policy Environment for Rural Non Farm Sector in India. Institute of Development Studies, Jaipur, September 10-11.

Krueger Anne C (1874): The Political Economy of Rent Seeking Society, The American Economic Review, June, p. 291-303.

Kurien C.T. (1978): Small Sector in New Industrial Policy, Economic and Political Weekly, March 4, pp. 455-461.

Little, Ian M.D., Dipak Majumdar and John M Page, Jr. (1987): Small Manufacturing Enterprises: A comparative analysis of India and other Economics, Oxford University Press, pp. 1-282.

Mendels Franklin (1872): Proto-Industrialisation: The first Phase of the Industrialisation process, Journal of Economic History, No. 1, Vol. 20, March, pp. 51-73.

Mohan Rakesh (1993): Industrial Location Policies and their implications for India, Studies in Industrial Development, Page No. 9, Ministry of Industry, New Delhi, pp. 1-34.

Nanjundan S (1994): Changing Role of Small Scale Industry: International influences, Country Experiences and Lessons for India, Economic and Political Weekly, Vol. 29, No. 22, May pp. M46-M53.

Nasir Tyabji (1989): The Small Industries Policy in India, Oxford University Press, Calcutta, pp. 1-203.

NCAER (1993): Structure and Promotion of Small Scale Industries in India—Lessons for Future Development, NCAER and FRIEDRIC –NAUMANN – STIFTUNG, New Delhi, pp. 1-315.

Panditrao Y.A. (1994): Experiences of the Khadi and Village Industries Commission in Technology Transfer, in Bhalla and Reddy (1994) (ed.). The Technological Transformation of Rural India, ILO-WEP, Intermediate Technology Publications, London.

Rapola T.S. and Mishra V. (1000): Some aspects of Rural Industrialisation, Economic and Political Weekly, Vol. 15, Nos. 41, 42 and 43, Special No. October pp. 1733, 1718.

Saith Ashwani (1998): Location, Linkage and Leakage: Malaysian Rural Industrialisation Strategies in National Perspective, Institute of Social Studies, Hague, WP series No. 56, pp. 1-68.

Sandesara J.C. (1992): Industrial Policy and Planning 1947-1991, Tendencies, Interpretations and Issues, Sage Publications, New Delhi, pp. 1-179.

Sandesara J.C. (1993): Modern Small Industry—1972 and 1967–88, Aspects of growth and Structural Change, Economic and Political Weekly, February 6, pp.

Sandesara J.C. (1996): Strategies for Employment Promotion: Search for an employment Growth Strategy. Economic and Political Weekly, May, 26, pp. 1161-1162.

Sandesara J.C. (1996): Small Industry in India: Evidences and Interpretation, Presidential address, Gujarat Economic Association, Ahamedabad.

Eanthanam Committee (1984): Report on the Committee on Prevention of Corruption, Government of India, Ministry of Home Affairs, New Delhi.

Uribe Francisco—Echevarria (1991): Small Scale Manufacturing and Regional Industrialisation: The Urban Region Development: Perspective, Institute of Social Studies, Hague, WP Series No. 116, pp. 1-50.

Uribe Francisco-Echevarria (1992): Small Scale Manufacturing and Regional Industrialisation: The Urban Region Development: Perspective, Institute of Social Studies, Hague, WP Series No. 117, pp. 1-59.

Sigurdson Jon (1979): Rural Industrialisation: A Comparison of Development Planning in China and India. World Development, Vol. No. 6, pp. 667-680.

Vaidyanathan A (1991): Cottage and Small Industry in India—Policy and Performance. Sir Purshotamdas Thakurdas Memorial Lecture. Indian Institute of Bankers.

Vaidyanathan A (1986): Labour use in Rural India: A study of spatial and temporal variations. Economic and Political Weekly, Vol. 21 No. 52, December, pp. A 130-A 146.

Vinod Vyasulu (1987): Development of Backward Areas, Yatan Publications, New Delhi pp. 17-89.

Vinod Vyasulu (1992): The non farm sector in the Indian Economy, Towards a long term Research Programme in Rural Industrialisation, RBI Units, ISRO Bangalore-72.

Vinod Vyasulu and Pandey A N (1986): Industrial Policy for backward areas. Indian Journal of Development Banking.

Vyas V.S. and Mathai George, 1985: Farm and Non-Farm Employment in Rural Areas: A Perspective for Planning, Economic and Political Weekly, Annual Number, February pp. 334-337.

FOOT NOTES

1. United Nations Organisation Report on "The Process and Problems of Industrialisation in under-Developed Countries". New York, United Nations, 1955, p. 16.

2. Gunnar Myrdal, "An International Economy", New York Horper and Brother, 1956, p. 226.

3. Ibid, p. 226.

4. C. Ganguli, "Studies in Indian Economic Problems, Calcutta, 1979, p. 1.

5. National Institute of Small Industry Extension Training Industrial Policy Resolution, Hyderabad, 1980. p. 2.

6. Ibid. p. 8.

7. For details on data sources and limitations of this sector see the paper on "Rural Industrialization"

8. The concept Proto Industrialization owes its Origin to Franklin Mendels, 1972.

9. The National Development Council (May 6th, 1955) in its meetings agreed to strengthen the village and small scale industries on an adequate scale in connection with the second five year plan. Thus, Karve Comitee was appointed to suggest measures to equip the sector to carry out the tasks assigned to it during the second plan and in the future.

10. The total public sector outlay to the small scale and village industry was 17 per cent, which was one of the highest shares during the entire plan period.

11. For details of the recommendations and implications of Pandey and Wanchoo Committee reports see Vyasula and Pandey, 1986.

12. For detailed description of the efficiency aspect of small scale sector see Framcico uribe Echevarria, 1991 and 1992.

13. At present the total number of items reserved for exclusive procurement purchase are 412. Some of these items are from the village industrial sector also.

14. The Santhanam Committee, 1964, started "Corruption has been increasing and that much of the blame lies with the prediferation of economic controls following independence page 7-8 for details of rent seeking activity see Krueger, 1974.

15. The compound Annual Rate of growth of the traditional sector during the period 1973-1974 to 1984-1985 was 4.5 per cent in terms of employment and 4.2 per cent in terms of production. During this period productivity of the sector shows a negative annual growth of 2 per cent. Thus the over all relative dominance in the generation of employment is slowly coming down, one best example is the handloom sector. At the same time the small scale sector showed better performance. The annual compound growth was 7.7 per cent 10.1 per cent in terms of employment and production respectively, and annual compound growth rate of productivity was 2.9 per cent. (Source government of India Planning Commission. The seventh five year plan 1985-90, Vol, II October 1985 pp. 99-103.

16. See the paper on "Rural Industrialization in India Khadi and Village Industries. Aspects of employment, production and disbursement" see also Vinod Vyasulu, 1992, A research programme in the Non-Form Sector, ISEC, Bangalore.

17. The sales of the village and small industry to the total of all heads was 2.1 per cent during the First plan. Increased to 4 per cent during the second plan. This one of the highest share even in the planned development. After that, the figures began to decline to 2.8 per cent during the third plan and 1.9 per cent during annual plans. The share in the fourth and fifth plan was 1.5 per cent each and since then it began to fluctuate between 1.6 and 1.8 per cent. In the seventh plan the share was 1.5 per cent.

18. For different views express in this direction see recent articles in Economic and Political Weekly.

19. Conference on Science and Technology in India; Retrospect and Prospect 13th Nov. 1985, Indian National Science Academy, New Delhi.

20. Boken J.S. et al., No limits to learning. A report to the club of Rome 1979.

21. Streelkerk Hein, Industrial Transition in Rural India, Artisans, Traders and Tribals in South Gujarat, Bombay Popular Prakashan, 1985.

22. Government of India.

23. National Productivity Council, 1999, "Rural Artisans in Payyammur Report of a study sponsored by the Inter Agency Coordination Committee for decentralized sector p. 31.

24. Hagela, Jitendara Kumar, "Village Worker and Technology Diffusion". The Indian Experience Manpower Journal Vol. XXXII No. 14 January-March, 1997, p. 59.

25. Parthasarathy R. "Economic Status and Labour Allocations Strategy of Rural Artisans Households in Gujarat Working Paper Series". Gujarat Institute of Development Research.

26. Vyas V., "Clay Industry of Gujarat State" A proposed case study for appropriate technology" paper presented at all-India Seminar on Rural Technology for village artisans Rural Technology Institute, Gandhi Nagar, Gujarat 12-15, February.

27. Jammu P.S. 1974, "Changing Social Structure in Rural Pubjab", Sterling Publishers Pvt., Ltd., New Delhi.

28. Centre for Studies in Decentralized Industries, 1983, "A Study of nature and causes of poverty among Rural Artisans Blacksmiths of Maharashtra State, Yavatmal District", Varkunt Bhai Mehta Samarak Trust, Bombay.

29. Solanki S.S., 1997, "Technology and the Indian Artisans Kurukshetra", Vol. XLV No. 12, September.

30. C. Ganguli Studies in India Economic Problems, Calcutta, 1978, p. 81.

31. M. Thimmaraju, "A case study of Rural Artisans of Chennapatna (Master Degree Dissertation), 1984, p. 1.

32. Government of Karnataka, "Artisans and their Credit needs in Karnataka", March. 1976.

33. S.C. Varma, Role of Khadi and Village Industries in Poverty Alleviation, 1981, p. 2.

34. Ibid, p. 3.

3

Kurnool District—A Profile

Kurnool District derives its name from its chief town, Kurnool, capital of Nawabs in the past and headquarters of the district at present. The name Kurnool is said to have been derived from KANDENAVOLU forming part of Rayalaseema.

Kurnool district is one of the oldest districts of Andhra Pradesh.

Location

The district is located geographically between 14° - 54' and 16° - 11' of the Northern Latitude and 96° - 58' and 78° - 25' of the Eastern longitude. It is bounded on the north by the Perennial Tungabhadra and Krishna rivers, and by Mahaboobnagar district, on the South by Anantapur and Cuddapah districts on the East by Prakasam district, on the West by Karnataka State.

Area

At present Kurnool District comprises 54 Revenue Mandals and 53 Mandal Praja Parishads with three administrative divisions. The district has an area of 17,658 Sq. kms. Amounting to 6.4 per cent of the total State area. Six types of soils are present. Black, Clay, Black Loam, Black Sandy, Red Sandy, Red Loam and Red Clay, Black Clay, Red Loam and Sandy Soils however account for over 78 per cent of the area.

Hill Ranges

The Nallamalas and the Erramalas constitute the principal hill ranges of the district. The nallamalas lying about 113 kms in the district, extend southward into Cuddapah District, and Northward into Mahaboobnagar district beyond the Krishna. The Erramalas, beginning in Cuddapah district run northward almost upto Kurnool town.

Climate

The district falls in the tropical zone. From February temperatures begin to rise rapidly and by May the mean maximum daily temperature is 40.8°C and the mean daily minimum temperature is 27.9°C. During the winter months, the mean daily temperature varies from 30.3°C to 16.1°C.

Rainfall

The district generally receives a fair amount of rainfall of about 620 mm per annum. The distribution of the rainfall is however widely scattered and unevenly spaced. Nearly 68 per cent of the rainfall is received during the South West monsoon.

Rivers

The principal rivers watering the district are the Tungabhadra and its tributary the Handri and the Krishna and the Konderu. While the Tungabhadra and the Krishna are perennial in nature, the Konderu is purely seasonal. The Tungabhadra rising in the Western ghats, flows for a length of 161 kms. in the district, while the Krishna rising in the Mahabaleswar hills, flows for a length of 165 kms. The Konderu rises in the Western side of the Erramalas. It flows in southern direction, collects the drainage in its course and passes through Nandikotkur, Nandyal, Allagadda and Koilkuntla before entering Cuddapah District. Besides there are 540 tanks serving as the main source of irrigation in the district.

The Hundri, a tributary of the Tungabhadra rises in the fields of Maddikera in Pattikonda taluk receives a stream from the Erramalas at Laddagiri in Kodumur mandal and joins the Tungabhadra at Kurnool. It drains much of Pattikonda taluk and portions of Dhone; Kodumur and

Kurnool taluks. This is a turbid stream with sudden rise and fall.

Administrative Setup

Administratively, the district is divided into 3 divisions (Kurnool, Adoni and Nandyal) consisting of 54 Mandals. In addition to Municipal Corporation at Kurnool, there are three Municipalities in the district at Nandyal, Adoni, and Yemmiganur. The district has 918 revenue Villages administered by 821 Gram Panchayats.

Population

As per 2001 census the district has a population of 35.11 Lakh. 17.87 Lakh males and 17.24 Lakh females. Rural population, constituting 74.2 per cent is predominant. Urban population is only 25.8 per cent. The density of population in the district is 168 per Sq. km. whereas the State average is 242 per Sq. Km. It is important to note that composition of urban population increased by 1.8% between 1991 and 2001 while there had been corresponding decline in rural population. The average literacy level among the district is 32.4 per cent, whereas the state average is 36.8 per cent. The occupational distribution of the population is as follows:

Table 3.1: The Occupational Distribution of the Population in Kurnool District

Sl. No.	*Type of Workers*	*No. of lakhs*		
		Rural	*Urban*	*Total*
1.	Main Workers	10.98	2.43	13.41
2.	Cultivators	3.22	0.10	3.32
3.	Agricultural Labourers	6.15	0.49	6.64
4.	Household Industry	0.18	0.13	0.31
5.	Other Main Workers	1.43	1.70	3.13
6.	Marginal Workers	0.39	0.03	0.42
7.	Non-Workers	10.67	5.23	15.91

The composition of SCs, STs; and Minorities in the district population is as follows:

Table 3.2: The Composition of SCs, STs and Minorities in the District Population

Sl. No.	*Category*	*No. of lakhs*		
		Rural	*Urban*	*Total*
1.	Scheduled Castes	4.16	1.02	5.18
2.	Scheduled Tribes	0.45	0.11	0.56
3.	Minorities	2.79	2.58	5.37

Major Economic Activities

Agriculture, Mining, Household Industry, Servicing, Manufacturing, Trade and Commerce constitute the major economic activities in the district.

Principal Crops	Groundnut, Cotton, Sunflower, Paddy, Mulberry, Sugarcane
Principal Horticulture Product	Mango, Banana, Papaya, Guava, Jasmine
Major Minerals	Limestone, Steatite, White Shale, Yellow Ochre, Dolomite, Quartz, Iron Ore, Silica
Household Industry	Carpentry, Pottery, Tanning, Footwear Making, Embroidery Dyeing and Printing, Silk Reeling.
Small Industry	Agri Based, Mineral Based, Forest, Engineering Based, Textile Based, Manufacturing Activities.
Large Industry	Cotton Yarn, Cement, Edible Oil, Caustic Soda, Sugar.
Servicing Activities	Repair of domestic electrical and other appliances. Servicing of Electrical Motors, Diesel Engines, Automobile Repairing, Tailoring, Computerised Data Processing, Telephone Booths, Typewriting.

Trade Activities	A wide range of consumer durables and non durables, food grains, seeds, fertilizers and machinery components.
No. of Large Scale Units	25
Investment	Rs.432.58 crores
Employment	Rs.10,327/-
No. of Registered Small Scale Units	3989
Investment	Rs.64.45 crores
Employment	Rs.22,870/-
Industrial Estates	Located at Kurnool, Adoni, Dhone and Nandyal

Natural Resources

Kurnool is endowed with a variety of natural resources, significantly the mineral sources, others include live stock, agricultural and forest resources.

Mineral Resources

Kurnool is one of the mineral rich districts of Andhra Pradesh. It is endowed with extensive deposits of cement grade lime stone. It abounds in a variety of building stones. Besides barytes, iron ore, clays, ochres, slate, steatite, saline efflorescence and quartz occur though relatively in small quantities.

Limestones occurs around Koilkuntla, Banganapalle, Dhone, Nandikotkur, Bethamcherla, Gadivemula, Panyam and Owk. The estimated reserves of limestone in the district aggregate around 8000 Million Tonnes.

Barytes of various grades occurring mainly around Bethamcherla, Kallur and Gadivemula find use in paint industry and in oil drilling operations. While clays are found extensively around Nandyal, Betamcherla and Pulicherla, Iron Ore (Haematite) occurs in the district, particularly in the Ramallakota-Veldurthy areas. An estimated size of the deposits is over 3.6 million tonnes. Considerable quantities of red oxide are estimated to occur in the Ramallakota – Veldurthy and Betamcharla areas. Saline efforescence occurs in a small way around Koilkuntla. Similarly deposits of steatite occur around Muddavaram, while large deposits of yellow ochre do near Bethamcherla, Ambapuram, Ramallakota and Uyyalawada. Deposits of slate occur in a large measure around Markapur, once part of Kurnool district, now of Prakasam district.

Land Utilisation Pattern

The Land Utilisation Pattern, Revenue Division wise in the District is as follows: - (As on 2001)

Table 3.3: Revenue Division-wise Land Utilisation Pattern in Kurnool District

Sl. No.	*Utilisation*	*Revenue Division*			
		Kurnool	*Nandyal*	*Adoni*	*Total*
(a)	Total Geographical Area	16.42	13.46	13.61	43.49
(b)	Area under Forests	3.63	3.77	0.46	7.86
(c)	Barren and Uncultivable Land	1.18	0.60	0.67	2.45
(d)	Land put to Non-Agricultural Uses	1.02	0.59	0.88	2.49
(e)	Permanent Pastures for Grazing	0.05	0.02	0.03	0.10
(f)	Miscellaneous Tree Crops and Groves	0.05	Neg	Neg	0.05
(g)	Cultivable Lands	0.86	0.72	0.44	2.02
(h)	Other Fallow Lands	1.69	1.00	0.79	3.48
(i)	Current Fallow Lands	1.05	0.97	0.85	2.87
(j)	Net Area Sown	6.89	5.79	9.48	22.16

Agricultural Resources

The Gross Cropped Area of the district during 2000-2001 is 10.04 lakh hectares and the net cropped area is 9.01 lakh hectares. Of this the net Irrigated area amounts to only 1.52 lakh hectares jowar, paddy and bazra are the principal food crops while groundnut, cotton, sunflower and tobacco are the major cash crops. The area under cultivation and the estimated production levels of these crops are as below:

Table 3.4: Estimated Production Levels of these Crops

Figures in lakhs.

Crop	*Area (Hectares)*	*Production (Tonnes)*
Jowar	1.61	2.09
Paddy	0.75	1.84
Barja	0.17	0.13
Groundnut	3.44	2.72
Tobacco	0.15	0.17
Cotton	0.88	0.21 (Bales)

Agriculture sector in the district assumes significance as the single largest employer. Besides, it supports a number of agri-produce processing activities, importantly paddy milling, edible oil extraction, flour milling, pulses processing, manufacture of sugar etc. It also sustains directly and indirectly activities such as fabrication and servicing of agricultural implements, maintenance of farm machinery and borewells.

The growth of the agricultural sector is however impeded mainly by meagre irrigation facilities and tiny land holdings.

Horticulture

About 5 per cent of the geographical area of the district is under various horticulture crops. The potential for horticulture produce in different mandals is as follows:

Sericulture

Sericulture activities, particularly mulberry cultivation and cocoon rearing, have picked up in the district considerably in the recent years. Some 4900 acres is under mulberry. The quantity of cocoons reared is around 9.50

Table 3.5: Horticulture Produce in Different Mandals of the Kurnool District

Sl. No.	*Horticulture Crops*	*Intensive*	Semi-Intensive	Less Intensive
1.	Mango	Kallur, B.Atmakur, Orvakal, Kodumur, Banaganapalli, Veldurthi.	Laddagiri Panyam Peapully	Nandyal, Gospadu, Serivella, Alur, Gadivemula, Gudur, Miduthur, Nandikotkur.
2.	Coconut	-NIL-	Orvakal	Atmakur
3.	Citrus	Kallur, Dhone, Kurnool.	Nandyal, Gudur, Krishnagiri.	Sirivella, Mahanandi, Kodumur, Dhone, Gudur, Veldurthi.
4.	Banana	Nandyal, Mahanandi	Orvakal	-
5.	Guava	Kallur, Kodumur	-	-
6.	Sapota	Panyam, Kallur, Govardanagiri	-	-
7.	Papaya	Nandyal Allagadda	Rudravaram, Goispadu, Chagalamarri.	Peapully, Kallur, Gadivemula.
8.	Jasmine	Kallur, Dhone, Nandyal, Panyam, Gospadu.	Kodumur, Banaganapalli, Kurnool, Atmakur, Koilakuntla.	-

lakh kgs. Silk reeling is not carried out in a significant way though there exists a good growth potential in this sector.

Live Stock and Poultry Resources

Kurnool is one of the richest districts in Andhra Pradesh as regards livestock. The population of bovine cattle is concentrated mainly around Dhone and Adoni and that of poultry around Nandyal and Markapur. In recent years the live stock population in Nandyal division has shown remarkable improvement. The live stock resources of the district are estimated as follows:

Table 3.6: Livestock Resources of the Kurnool District

Livestock	*Lakh Heads 2001*
Animals	
Cattle	4.80
Buffaloes	3.82
Sheep	4.85
Goats	2.12
Horses or Ponie	0.01
Pigs	0.15
Fowls and Ducks	9.10
Poultry	15.83
Others	0.08

Forest Resources

The district has a thick forest cover. The total area under forests is 7,86,412 acres it is about 20 per cent of the total geographical area of the district. The major parts of the forest area are confined mainly to the Nallamalas, the Erramalas and a part of the Velikondas. The Forests of the Erramalas and the Velikondas are of interior type.

Bamboo with timber species occur fairly over extensive areas in the district. Tamarind and Beedi leaves are the important minor forest produce of the district.

The forest wealth of the district has facilitated in the establishment of number of saw mills and wooden furniture manufacturing units. The wood from the forest is used not only in the manufacture of wooden furniture but also in making construction items like doors, windows and agricultural implements, cabinets, carts, baskets etc. The forest with its immense wealth provides many of working class with avenues of employment such as felling, logging, transport of timber, collection of minor forest produce and forest based industries like basket making, rope making, leaf plates making, mat weaving etc.

The district forest yields different species of timber, the prominent ones being Yepi Chiriman, Vepa, Yegisa, Nallamaddi, Bandaru and Bamboo. Besides, the minor produce includes tamarind, soapnuts, latefolia, karaka, beedi leaves etc.

Infrastructure Facilities

The Physical Infrastructure available in the district comprises road, rail, transportation, power, and telecommunication facilities.

Roads

Kurnool District has a well-developed and reliable road network. All the towns and almost all the villages are connected with dependable all weather roads. The district has access to national highway as Kurnool town falls on NH7 between Hyderabad and Bangalore.

The road network comprises cement concrete, black topped metalled and bumetalled roads of a total length of over 6000 km cement, black topped and metalled roads constitute nearly 76 per cent of the roads in the district.

Rail

The district enjoys regular rail facilities. The district head quarters is connected with Hyderabad in the North, and Tirupati in South and Nandyal in the East, Hubli in the West. The route kilometerage of railways in the district aggregates around 300 kms.

Transportation

Transportation of people and goods in the district is carried through a well developed organised and easily accessible network of trains, buses, taxies and goods carriers.

Power

The only power generation source in the district is the Srisailam Hydro Electric Power Generation Project with an installed capacity of 9,770 M.W.

Telecommunications

The Telecommunication network in the district consists of Telephone, Telegraph and Postal facilities. There are 815 Post Offices, 254 Telegraph Offices and 101 Telephone Exchanges. All the important places enjoy dependable STD and ISD facilities.

Industrial Estates

In order to provide dependable infrastructure facilities, especially to small scale units the Government has developed industrial estates around Kurnool, Adoni, Dhone and Nandyal Towns. Besides, with central government assistance, an Industrial Infrastructure Development Centre (IIDC) project has also been set up at Nandyal. Details of the number of Industrial Plots and Sheds developed in these estates and the vacancy positions are given:

The social infrastructure available includes banking, education and medicare facilities.

Banking

The banking system is well established and entrenched in the district serving different strata of people. There are 210 bank branches – 32 Commercial Bank Branches, 59

Grameena Bank Branches and 19 Co-operative Bank Branches and others.

The credit flow to various sectors from the banks during 2000-2001 aggregated Rs.143.46 crores against a target of Rs.192.39 crores as detailed below.

Table 3.7: The Credit Flow to Various Sectors in Kurnool District

Sector	*Target*	*Achievement*	*% Achievement*
Crop Loans	9203.83	8814.19	95.77
Term Loans	3875.93	1478.64	38.15
SSI Loans	2887.17	1893.60	65.58
Territory	3271.92	2159.36	66.00
Total	19238.85	14345.79	74.57

Education and Training

The district has facilities for primary, middle, secondary, collegiate, vocational and professional education. There are 72 Colleges, including, Junior Colleges, Polytechnics, ITI's, Medical College, Engineering College and S.K. University P.G. Centre. A reasonable base has developed over the years in the district for imparting vocational skills to the youth. Polytechnics and privately owned skill training institutes impart skills in the areas of Radio and TV repairs, electrification, automobile repairs, motor rewinding, computer data processing, wool spinning, terrakota pottery, silk reeling, kalamkari printing, dyeing and printing, making of soft toys, garment designing and fabric weaving.

Medicare

The district has a wide network for medical facilities comprising hospitals (17), dispensaries (16) and primary health centres (58) with an aggregate bed strength of 1519. Facilities are available for clinical treatment, surgery and eyecare.

Industrial Development in Kurnool

Kurnool is regarded as an Industrially backward district. The rate of Industrial development is relatively low, though several measures have been initiated to accelerate Industrial development in the district. These include offering investment subsidies, providing industrial infrastructure, extending vocational training support and offering concessional finances, especially to the small and tiny units.

The existing industrial scene in the district is dotted by the presence of a relatively small number of large and medium scale units a fairly large number of registered small scale units and a very large number of unregistered non-farm sector units.

Large and Medium Scale Units

There are presently 25 large and medium scale units in the district with an estimated aggregate capital investment of Rs.435.46 crores and employing over 10,000 persons. A list of the large and medium scale, units set up in the district as given in Annexure—III. Activity wise distribution of these units points to the dominance of chemical and agro based units followed by textile, food and mineral based units as detailed below:

Table 3.8: Activity-wise Distribution of Large and Medium Scale Units in Kurnool District

Sl. No.	*Category*	*Units*	*Investment Rs. Crores*	*Employment Nos.*
1.	Chemical	5	206.36	598
2.	Agro	4	130.04	781
3.	Textile	3	12.90	2477
4.	Mineral	2	36.88	910
5.	Food	4	15.15	2023
	Total	18	401.33	6789

Note: Sick Units Omitted.

The chemical based units are engaged in the manufacture of a wide variety of basic chemical like caustic soda, liquid, chlorine, hydrochloric acid, staple bleaching powder, high strength hypochlorate, calcium carbide, oxygen and LPG bottling.

The agro based units relate to edible oil, extraction and refining of writing and printing paper and crystal sugar manufacturing. While the textile based units, the mineral based units are engaged mainly in the manufacture of portland cement, the food based units are engaged in diverse activities as vanaspati manufacturing, processing of liquid milk and soft drinks bottling. It is however important to note that though a majority of the large and medium units in the district are continuously processing units, their contribution to the development of the small scale auxiliaries seems to be low.

The geographical spread of these units points to locational concentration in and around Kurnool. Adoni, Nandyal and Yemmiganur towns. Further the locational choice seems to have been guided more by proximity to raw material sources. Field level discussions indicate that only 50 per cent of the large and medium units are functioning well. Of the remaining a majority are limping while the rest were declared as sick units and ceased functioning.

Small Scale Units

There are 3,989 registered small scale units in the district with an estimated aggregated investment of Rs. 64.45 crores and providing employment to 22.870 persons. This is as per the statistics of March 2001.

Activitywise distribution of these units reveals the predominance of mineral based units followed by agro, forest, engineering, chemical and food based units. The activity wise distribution of SSI in Kurnool district is as follows:

Cuddapah slab polishing units, rice shellers, dal mills, ground nut decorticators, oil expellers and rotaries predominate the small industry scene in the district.

Table 3.9: Activity-wise Distribution of SSIs Units in Kurnool District

Sl. No.	*Activity*	*Units*	*Investment Rs.Lakhs*	*Employment Nos.*
1.	Agro Based	754	1605.14	4,735
2.	Mineral Based	1,035	1,542.97	7,130
3.	Food Based	120	69.87	1,804
4.	Chemical Based	188	831.08	1,804
5.	Engg. Based	576	508.63	2,435
6.	Leather Based	45	15.05	195
7.	Textile Based	25	30.85	153
8.	Forest Based	317	116.82	1,288
9.	Miscellaneous	929	612.57	3,124
	Total	3,989	6,444.95	22,870

Other Important lines of activity include P.V.C. Pipes manufacturing, roller flour milling, manufacture of instant foods, pharmaceuticals, detergents, readymade garments, bricks, paper, cones, warping and sizing of yarn, pulverising of minerals, char coal manufacturing, wooden furniture and general engineering workshop, footwear manufacturing etc.

The geographical distribution of the SSI units in the district reveals a relative concentration of these units in the mandals of Nandyal, Kurnool, Adoni, Dhone, Kallur, Bethamcherla, Kolimigundila, Atmakur and Yemmiganur.

While the overall performance of the SSI units in the district is reportedly satisfactory, there are 40 sick SSI units distributed over a cross section of manufacturing activities.

Unregistered Tiny Units

In addition to the registered small and tiny units, there are a sizeably large number of unregistered tiny units engaged in handloom weaving and a myriad manufacturing, processing, servicing and trading activities. No reliable data is available regarding the number of such units, investments made in them, employment generated, business turnovers etc.

The unregistered tiny units however make a significant contribution to the district economy, especially from the view-point of providing lasting self-employment avenues to artisans and educated unemployed.

Artisan Industries

Nallamala Forest of Kurnool District has been supplying enough raw material for the development of carpentry and Bamboo basket making Industry. This is the reason why these Industries are very well developed in Kurnool District. Blacksmith, Cobblery and Goldsmith industries are also well developed in this district.

Government Initiatives for Self-Employment Promotion

Several policy measures have been initiated for the promotion of self-employment and entrepreneurship among different target groups through the establishment of specific institutions and launching of several schemes. Mention could be made in this regard of measures such as extending margin money support, investment subsidy, composite loans and concessional finances.

Among the institutions catering to the growth of small business and entrepreneurship are the DIC, Scheduled Caste Co-operative Finance Corporation, Backward Classes Finance Corporation. District Rural Development Agency (DRDA), AP Minorities Finance Corporation and Commissionerate of Youth Services.

Prime Minister's Rojgar Yojana: (PMRY)

PMRY, a Central Government sponsored programme, aims at promotion of self-employment and entrepreneurship among educated unemployed youth primarily through imparting entrepreneurial training and extension of financial assistance upto 1.00 Lakhs per beneficiary to help setup tiny manufacturing servicing and trading ventures. A total of 2431 beneficiaries were offered support in Kurnool District under PMRY during 1993-1994 to 2000-2001 years.

Chief Minister's Employment of Youth Programme

Chief Minister's Employment of Youth Programme was launched during 1996-97 to help rural youth to form into cohesive groups and take to viable economic activities. During 1996-1997 a total of 391 youth groups were formed in the district and tiny units established to undertake a wide range of group of economic activities.

Assistance by S.C. Corporation

Scheduled Caste Cooperative Finance Corporation also has been extending financial assistance through provision of Margin Money and term loans from NSFDC to potential entrepreneurs belonging to scheduled castes. During 1995-1998 and 2000-2001 financial assistance was extended to more than 2000 beneficiaries in the district to enable them to set up self employment ventures.

Assistance by B.C. Corporation

Andhra Pradesh Backward Classes Co-operative Finance Corporation has been extending financial assistance to potential entrepreneurs among backward classes through provision of margin money and term loans under NBCFDC. During 1998-1999 to 2000-2001 nearly 1800 beneficiaries availed assistance to set up their own small self employment ventures.

The promotional measures initiated thus far have made a positive impact on the promotion of self-employment in the district. Nevertheless the existing pattern of opportunity preference by beneficiaries shows an excessive degree of preference towards conventional and business activities. It would therefore be imperative to promote more of manufacturing and servicing activities.

ANNEXURE—I

Table 3.10: Major Minerals Occurring in Kurnool District

Sl.No.	*Name of the Mandal*	*Name of the Village*	*Mineral Available*
1.	Bethamcherla	Guttapalli	Limestone
		Ambapuram	Yellow Ochre
		Kolumulapalli	Steatite
		M. Pendekallu	Steatite
		Emboi RF	Steatite
		Muddavaram	Steatite
		RS Rangapuram	Steatite, Limestone
		Balapalapalli	Steatite
		Bethamcherla	Steatite, White Clay White Shale
		Gorlagutta	Limestone Slabe (Napa Slabs)
		Kothapalli	-do-
		Rangapuram	-do-
		Emboi	-do-
		Bugganipalli	-do-
		Kothapalli R	-do-
2.	Dhone	Malkapuram	Limestone, Mossaic Chips
		Valasala	-do-
		Kocheruvu	-do-
		P. Malkapuram	Limestone, Steatite, Wile Shale
		Racherla	Limestone
			Mossaic Chips
		Kothapalli	Mossaic Chips
3.	Gadivemula	Gadiverevula	Lime Stone
		Gani RF	Lime Stone
			Barytes, White Shale
4.	Kolimigundla	Kanakadripalli	Lime Stone (Cement Grade)
		Petnikota	-do-
		Itikala	-do-
		Petnikota	Limestone Slabs
		Thummalaopenta	-do-
		Belum	-do-
		Chintalayapalli	-do-
		Abdullapuram	-do-
		Meerjapuram	-do-
		Anki Reddy Palli	-do-
		Kurumanipalli	-do-
		Ktikala	-do-

(Contd...)

Sl.No.	*Name of the Mandal*	*Name of the Village*	*Mineral Available*
5.	**Kodumur**	Gorantla	Quartz
6.	**Orvakal**	Orvakal	Quarry Silica Sand
		Chintalayapalli	-do-
		Purecherla	-do-
		Kalva	-do-, Barytes
		Boidduvanipalli	Steatite
		Komarolu	White Shale
		Meedivemula	Quartz & Silica Sand
		Ketavaram	Limestone Slabs
		Uyyalawada	-do-
		Brahmanapalli	-do-
7.	**Adoni**	Mandagiri	Road Metal
		S. Kondapuram	-do-
		Bychigiri	-do-
		Kapati	Granite (Pink)
		Billekalu	-do-
		Doddanakallu	-do-
		Chinna Pentakal	-do-
		Arekallu	-do-
		Kuppagal	-do-
8.	Banaganapalli	Ramtirtham	Limestone
		Nandavaram	-do-
		Gulamaliabad RF	-do-
		Venkatapuram	White Clay
		Katikavanikuntla	Quartz & Silica Sand
		Palkur	Lime Stone Slabs
		Pathapadu	-do-
		Bhanumukkala	Road Metal
9.	Peapully	Chandrapalli	Limestone (High Grade)
		Nereducherla	-do-
		Jaladurgam	-do-
		Madavaram RF	-do-
		Peapully RF	-do-
		Burgula USHB	-do-
		Peddapaya RF	Barytes
		Utakonda	-do-
		Peddapodilla	-do-
		Kommemarri	White Shale, Steatite
		Rayampeta	-do-
		Peddapodilla	-do-
		Munimadugu	Limestone Mossaic Chips

Sl.No.	*Name of the Mandal*	*Name of the Village*	*Mineral Available*
		B. Cheruvupalle	-do-
		Racherla	-do-
		Nereducherla	-do-
		Burugula	-do-
10.	Kallur	Tadakanapalli	Limestone Mossaic Chips
		Yaparlapadu	Barytes
		K. Nagalapuram	Felsfer
		Ulindakonda	Limestone
		Ulchala	Limestone
11.	Krishnagiri	Chittalaya	Steatite
		Yerukalacheruvu	Black Granite
		Krishnagiri	Black Granite
12.	Panyam	Konidedu	Limestone (Cement Granite)
		Panyam RF	Slabs
		Alamur	Limestone
		Thamarajupalli	Road Metal
13.	Sirivella	Sirivella	Barytes
14.	Veldurthy	Koluguntla	Quartz Iron Ore
		Ramallakota	Yellow Ochre, Iron Ore
		Veldurthy	Iron Ore
		Sarparajapuram	Iron Ore
		Boyanapalli	Iron Ore
		Guntipalli	Road Metal
15.	Holagunda	Chinnahyta	Quartz
16.	Kurnool	Gargurapuram	Barytes
		Pudur	Steatite
		Panchalingala	Sand
17.	Midtur	Nagalooti	Limestone Slabs
		Peerusaheb Peta	-do-
18.	Peddakadabur	Rangapuram	Pink Granite
		Nowlekallu	-do-
		Peddakadabur	-do-
		Chinna Thubalam	-do-
19.	Yemmiganur	Kotakal	Pink Granite
		Devibetta	-do-
20.	Owk	Ramapuram	Limestone Slabs
		Cherlopalli	-do-
		Rangapuram	-do-

ANNEXURE—II

Table 3.11: Industrial Estates in Kurnool District

Sl. No.	Name of the Zone and Code No.	Land		Plots		Shed/Houses/Ocs						Rate of land cost Communicated during 4/95 Rs.	Rate of cost revi-with. effect from 15.09.95 Rs.
		Total Land Acres	Land Developed Acres	Un-Dev. land allotted Acres	Un-Dev. land vacent	Total No.	Allotted No.	Vacant No.	Total No.	Allotted No.	Vacant No		
I	Les/IDAs/APIEs/etc.												
1.	Kurnool	92.50	92.50	–	–	168 (58)	108 (44.70) Acres	58 (12.08) Acres	53 (5.33) Acres	47 (4.70) Acres	6 (0.63) Acres	150.00	125.00
2.	APIE-Adoni	28.51	28.51	–	–	41 (16) Acres	20 (9.7) Acres	21 (6.30) Acres	4 (1.11) Acres	4 (1.11) Acres	–	30.00	–
3.	IE-Dhone	29.75	–	29.75	–	73 (29.75) Acres	73 (29.75) Acres	NIL	–	–	–	15.00	–
4.	IE-Nandyal	23.83	23.83	–	–	25 (9.16) Acres	25 (9.16) Acres	NIL	24 (7.00) Acres	24 (7.00) Acres	–	125.00	–
5.	IIDC-Nandyal	68.55	–	68.55	–	–	92 (31.40) Acres	28 (21.64) Acres	64	–	–	125.00	–

ANNEXURE—III

Table 3.12: List of Large and Medium Scale Industries in Kurnool District

Sl. No.	Name of the Industry	Product Line	Installed Capacity	Total Capital Investment (Rs. Lakh)	Employment (No.)
1.	M/s. Sree Rayalaseema Alkalies and Allied Chemicals Ltd. Gondiparla, Kurnool	Caustic Soda	53000 TPA	12,311	46
		Liquid Chlorine	4650 TPA		
		Hydrochloric Acid	14840 TPA		
		Hydrogen Gas (100% Basis)	14000000 Cu Mt.		
		Sodium Hypochlorite (100% Basis)	1650 TPA		
		Hydrogenerated Castor Oil	16500 TPA		
		12 Hydroxy Stearic Acid	9900 TPA		
2.	M/s. Sree Rayalaseema Hi-Strength Hypo. Ltd., Gondiparla, Kurnool.	Staple Bleaching Powder	30 TPD	95	20
3.	M/s. Sree Rayalaseema Hi-Strength Hypo. Ltd., Gondiparla, Kurnool.	Sulphuric Acid	150 TPD	900	35
		Oleum	50 TPD		
		Chloro Sulphonic Acid	80 TPD		
4.	M/s. Sree Rayalaseema Hi-Strength Hypo. Ltd., Gondiparla, Kurnool.	Hi-Strength Hypo. Chlorite	15 TPD	630	30
5.	M/s. Modern Proteins Ltd. Kallur, Kurnool Dt.	Edible Oil and Solvent Extraction	17387 TPA	100	20

(Contd...)

Sl. No.	Name of the Industry	Product Line	Installed Capacity	Total Capital Investment (Rs. Lakh)	Employment (No.)
6.	M/s. AP Carbides Ltd. Dinnedevarapadu, Kurnool.	Calcium Carbide	23000 TPA	660	24
7.	M/s. Tungabhadra Industries Ltd. Kurnool.	Vanaspathi	88574 TPA	839	150
8.	M/s. Milk Product Factory Ayyalur, Nandyal	Liquid Milk	450 Lakh Lit.	364	303
9.	M/s. Annapurna Industries Ltd. Gajulapalli, Nandyal	Soft Drinks	428604 Crates	102.40	70
10.	M/s. The Nandyal Cooperative Sugar Mills Ltd. Ponnapuram, Nandyal	White Crystal Sugar	1250 TCD	822	609
11.	M/s. The Nandyal Cooperative Spinning Mills Ltd. Vaddugondla, Panyam	Cotton Yarn	25000 Spindles	630	439
12.	M/s. Panyam Cements and Mineral Industries Ltd. Cement Nagar, Bethamcherla, Kurnool District	Cement (OPC)	45099	3,612	741
13.	M/s. Bhagyalakshmi Vegetable Products Ltd. Adonil Kurnool Dist.	Vanaspathi Refined Oil	25 TPD 20 TPD	210	150
14.	M/s. Alimchand Topondas Oil Industries Ltd. Adoni.	Solvent Extraction (Vegetable Oil)	40131 TPD	160	250

Sl. No.	Name of the Industry	Product Line	Installed Capacity	Total Capital Investment (Rs. Lakh)	Employment (No.)
15.	M/s. Kothari Industries Corporation Ltd. Adoni.	Cotton Yarn	30000	850	760
16.	M/s. Adoni Cotton Mills, Adoni.	Cotton Yarn	20000	124	465
17.	M/s. The Rayalaseema Mills Ltd., Adoni	Cotton Yarn	36270	40	1089
18.	M/s. The Yemmiganur Spinning Mills Ltd., Yemmiganur.	Cotton Yarn	36008	398	628
19.	M/s. Adoni Oxygen Bottlers, Adoni.	Oxygen Gax		40	10
20.	M/s. ITC Agro Tech. Ltd. Tungabhadra, Mantralayam.	Mnfg. and refining of edible oil		7,500	100
21.	M/s. Raghavendra Prestressed Products Ltd. Tungabhadra Village, Mantralayam Mandal.	Prestressed Concrete Sleepers	213042	87.72	169
22.	M/s. S.V. Cements Ltd., Kankadripalli Village, Kolimigundla Mandal.	Portland Cement		288	275
23.	M/s. Nu-Tech Agros Ltd. Sadapuram Village, Adoni Mandal.	Deoiled Rice Bran	45000 TPA	83	128
24.	M/s. Bharat Petroleum Corpn. Laxmipuram Village, Kallur Mandal.	LPG Bottling Pland		6,700	50
			Total	43546	10327

4

Implementation of Adarana Scheme for Rural Artisans in Kurnool District

Introduction

Government of Andhra Pradesh has introduced Adarana Scheme for the first time in the state. Adarana (relief) – is a project pioneered to empower backward caste artisans in the State by providing improved hand tools, power tools and small technological equipment. An attempt is made in this chapter to spot light the overall performance of Adarana in Kurnool District.

Objectives

ADARANA: aims at providing modern and improved hand-held tools to the artisans with a view to improve their productivity, minimizing human drudgery, improving product/service quality and help modernise process operations. The ultimate goal is to contribute to increase income levels and improve standards of living of artisans.

The following guidelines are communicated to ensure effective implementation of ADARANA Project.

Occupational Groups Considered for Assistance

The major Occupational Groups identified for assistance along with their traditional activities are shown below:

Nature of Assistance

Only improved tools, technologies and equipment are provided under the project. Assets such as sheep and cattle

Table 4.1: The Major Occupational Groups Identified for Assistance along with their Trditional Activities

Sl. No.	*Occupational Groups*	*Major Economic Activity*	*Per cent share in the total Occupational group Population (State Level)*
1.	Yadava Golla Kuruma Kuruba	Cattle Rearing Milk Vending Sheep Rearing Kumbli Weaving	23.43%
2.	Gowda Ediga Settibalija Yata Gamaeler Gundla Kalalee Srisayana	Toddy Tapping	16.34%
3.	Agnikulakshatriya Besta Gangaputra Vanyakulakshatriya Vadda Balija Pattapu Jalari Palli Gangavaru Goondla Vannereddy Pallireddy Nayeelu	Fishing	9.34%
4.	Padmasali Devanga Thogata Thogati T.V. Kshatriya Patkar Swakulasali Jandra Atchukatla Vandlu	Weaving	9.24%
5.	Odde Uppara Vaddelu Sagaras	Earth Works	7.22%

(Contd...)

Sl. No.	Occupational Groups	Major Economic Activity	Per cent share in the total Occupational group Population (State Level)
6.	Vishwabrahmin Kamsali Kanchari Kammari Vadrangi	Goldsmithy Blacksmithy Brassmithy Stone Carving (Silpi) Carpentry	6.73%
7.	Rajaka	Laundry	11.88%
8.	Dudekula Noorbasha Luddaq Pinjaries	Cotton Carding	4.05%
9.	Kummara Kulala	Pottery	4.10%
10.	Nayeebrahmin Mangali	Hair Dressing	4.39%
11.	Gandla Telikula	Oil Pressing	1.17%
12.	Arekatika Katika	Butchery	0.87%
13.	Medari Gundala Gadaba	Basketry	0.64%
14.	Poosala	Petty Dealers (Beads & Needles)	0.22%
15.	Rangrej Chippolu/Mera Bhavasara Kshatriya	Tailoring/Dyeing	0.19%
			100%

and working capital requirements of the artisans are not to be considered.

Suggestive Activities

A list of indicative activities, occupational group-wise, was communicated to the District Collectors along with the physical targets and financial allocations. These activities are indicative in nature and Collectors are free to add any new activities which are artisan in nature under each occupational group. For example, activities such as plumbing, electrician, etc., can also be considered under different occupational groups, provided there is demand for the same and the artisans are currently pursuing them. But I.S.B. activities such as kirana shops, xerox machines and distribution of animals are not to be considered as part of the project.

Some of the occupational groups mentioned above may have diversified into activities not considered to be their traditional activities. For example, Dudekula community in Kurnool has taken to weaving and carpentry in addition to cotton carding, their traditional occupation. In such cases, new activities can also be considered eligible for assistance under the project in addition to the traditional artisan occupations.

However, in such cases the overall number of artisans targeted to be covered against a specific occupational groups, in a district will remain unchanged. For example, carpentry as an activity for Dudekula community could be considered within the overall number of beneficiaries intended to be covered under Dudekula community.

The allocations made to districts, both financial and physical, are shown occupation group wise. The Physical allocations made in terms of the number of beneficiaries to be covered are fixed, occupation group wise. The financial allocations are however, indicative as they may vary depending upon the unit costs.

For example, for one district under occupational group 'X', physical allocations are 1000 and the financial allocations Rs. 40.00 lakhs. However, depending upon the beneficiary's choice of tools the unit costs vary. As such, it is possible to cover all the 1000 beneficiaries within a financial allocation of Rs. 30.00 lakhs, instead of allocated Rs. 40.00 lakhs. Thus 1000 beneficiaries will be covered under occupational Group 'X' with an outlay of Rs. 30.00 lakhs only.

Like wise, in another occupational group 'Y' with a physical allocation of 1000 beneficiaries and financial allocation of Rs.20.00 lakhs, the financial outlay required could be Rs.30.00 Lakhs instead of Rs.20.00 lakhs depending upon the unit costs of the tools actually preferred by the beneficiaries.

The surplus of financial allocation in occupational group 'X' amounting to Rs.10.00 lakhs could be utilized to meet the additional financial allocation required to cover the 1000 beneficiaries with a higher unit cost in occupational group 'Y'.

After covering all the occupations group wise, as targeted, if still there are surplus funds left with the district B.C. Service Cooperative Society, they can be spent for other activities only after obtaining the prior approval of A.P. Backward Classes Cooperative Finance Corporation (APBCCFC) herein after referred to as Head Office.

The Occupational Group wise allocations communicated to the districts should be placed before District Development Review Committee (DDRC) for approval. If there are any Major Omissions in terms of B.C. communities whose activities are artisanal in nature, they may be included.

Funding Pattern

The funding pattern for assistance under the project is grouped into four categories as follows:

Table 4.2: The Funding Pattern for Assistance under the Project

Category	*Unit Cost*	*Funding Pattern*		
		Artisan Share	*Loan*	*Subsidy*
I.	Upto Rs. 2500/-	10%	10%	80%
II.	Rs. 2,501/- to 5,000/-	10%	20%	70%
III.	Rs. 5,001/- to 10,000/-	15%	35%	50%
IV.	Rs. 10,001/- to 20,000/-	15%	50%	35%

While assisting artisans under the project, care may be taken to conform to the following ratios for promoting different categories of units.

Table 4.3: Ratios for Promoting Different Categories of Units

Category	*Unit Cost*	*% of units to be assisted*
I.	Upto Rs. 2,500/-	37.5
II.	Rs. 2,501/- to Rs. 5,000/-	25.0
III.	Rs. 5,001/- to 10,000/-	25.0
IV.	Rs. 10,001/- to 20,000/-	12.5

Conforming to the above ratios will be essential to maintain the requisite balance in the funds flow through subsidy, loan and artisan contribution.

In respect of categories I and II, the loan to the beneficiaries will be provided by the A.P. Backward Classes Cooperative Finance Corporation (APBCCFC).

As regards categories III and IV, the loan component is to be tied up with the banks. All the banks concerned have been addressed by the SLBC to actively participate and extend loans to artisans under the project.

District Collectors are requested to pursue with the local banks for their full cooperation in grounding the project.

Units with unit costs between Rs. 20,000/- and Rs. 1,00,000/- could be considered group units. The ratio between artisan share, loan and subsidy in respect of such units would be the same as in the case of units with unit costs between Rs. 10,00/- and Rs. 20,00/- i.e., 15 per cent artisan share, 50 per cent loan and 35 per cent subsidy.

Where the unit cost under group activity exceeds Rs. 1.00 lakh, such cases could be considered only with the prior approval of Head Office.

Artisan's contribution will be collected at the time of grounding the unit.

Loan Repayment Schedule

Category I and II Units

Loan amount together with interest thereon is to be recovered by District B.C. Service Cooperative Societies as per guidelines to be issued separately by the Head Office.

Category III and IV Units

Loan amount together with interest thereon is repayable as per norms of the lending banks.

Beneficiary Identification

The beneficiary identification will be made in B.C. Artisan Grama Sabha to be held for a cluster of villages. A team led by Janmabhoomi Nodal Officer and consisting of MRO, MDO and any other officer of the rank of APO (DRDA). The Extension Officer (Industries) deputed by the Collector, representative of the bank concerned and the Sarpanches of the concerned Gram Panchayats concerned will select the beneficiaries. The local Self Help Group leaders will also assist the selection team.

In urban areas the municipal ward members or councillors will be members of the selection teams. Municipal Commissioner or his representative will be a member in place of MDO.

The beneficiary should be a practising B.C. artisan of the particular occupational group. In the case of toddy tappers, if there is a dispute whether or not one is a practising toddy tapper, help of the local toddy tappers society may be taken for deciding the selection.

Between two practising B.C. artisans from a particular occupational group, preference will be given to the poorer B.C. artisan.

Preference will also be given to those adopting family planning, sending children to school and participating actively in Janmabhoomi, Clean and Green and other Community Development Programmes.

White Ration Card holders alone will be eligible for units with a unit cost upto Rs.5,000/-. Those who do not possess white card can also be considered for units with unit cost upto Rs.5,000/-, provided it is established during the B.C. Artisan Grama Sabha that his/her family income is less than Rs.11,000/- per annum. For units with unit costs of above Rs.5,000/- all B.C. artisans are eligible. Only one beneficiary will be considered from one family of artisans.

Beneficiaries of the DRDA tool kit programme will not be eligible for units with a unit cost of less than Rs.5,000/-. However, they can be considered for units with unit costs of more than Rs.5,000/- if they fulfil the other criteria. Since the project is to be implemented over a 10 month period, the beneficiary selection is to be done in one sweep in the month of December 1998. During the course of the B.C. Artisan Grama Sabha, the total target beneficiaries to be covered under the project during 1998-1999 and 1999-2000 are selected. This is with reference to the State target of 10.00 lakhs beneficiaries.

Depending upon the district target for the 9 months period, the list of beneficiaries to be covered month wise is prepared at the meeting of B.C. Artisan Grama Sabha itself and beneficiaries are intimated the month in which their units are likely to be grounded, by issuing an Identification Slip.

A detailed plan of action for implementation has been worked out by the District B.C. Service Cooperative Societies based on the number of beneficiaries to be covered month wise. At the time of the beneficiary identification itself, beneficiaries' choice of tools will be ascertained and approximate unit cost arrived at, based on the tool costs furnished by the Head Office. All the beneficiaries will then be classified into four slabs on the lines of the funding pattern indicated above.

Documentation

An application form as prescribed will be filled in at the meeting of the B.C. Artisan Grama Sabha, the caste and income columns will be countersigned by the MRO at the time of filling up of the application, simultaneously.

In addition, form of Admission to the District B.C. Service Cooperative Society (along with a membership fee of Rs. 11/-) and Loan Bond Form need to be filled up by all the selected beneficiaries. The membership fee for admission to the B.C. Service Cooperative Society shall be paid at the time of selection.

Process of Grounding

For the purpose of grounding, all units under the project are broadly grouped as follows:

Group–I: These are units where the supply involves standard tools (e.g. Bicycle, brass iron, medlari chark etc.) and overall unit cost does not exceed Rs.2,500/-. The information about tools and equipment falling in this group will be passed on to the district officers. The choice of the brand can be ascertained from the beneficiary at the time of beneficiary selection to enable the District B.C. Service Cooperative Society to indent and procure the same. Other standard equipment to make the unit cost Rs.2,500/- can be locally purchased by District Collectors eg:- Milk cans with cycle, drums and buckets with iron-box to the washermen etc.

Group–II: In case of trades like carpentry there are a number of suppliers and a wide range of tools are available to choose from. To facilitate beneficiaries in this group to select the tools of their choice, Buyer Seller Meets for 500-1000 beneficiaries and Tools Suppliers will be organised. This is proposed for the trades of Carpentry, Stone Cutting, Blacksmithy.

Group-III: These are the trades and activities where the supply base is restricted or import of equipment is required. In these cases the information about the firms supplying the tools concerned is provided by the Head Office. In addition, if the beneficiaries concerned have any choice of firms for supplying the tools, it can also be considered and beneficiary choice should be obtained in identification camps. Wherever import is involved, APBCCFC will place orders.

Wherever import is not involved District B.C. Service Cooperative Societies will place orders as per beneficiaries choice.

It is also proposed to supply each beneficiary identification team with a video cassette containing information about various tools available, Occupational Group-wise, together with details of suppliers, product specifications, prices etc. The same may be screened to the beneficiaries and their choice obtained in respect of tools falling in groups I and III. For beneficiaries falling in Group II, video may be shown for their information. The actual selection of tools will be made only during Buyer Seller Meets.

Once the beneficiary's choice is obtained and the unit costs are arrived at, depending on the unit costs of tools, cases with unit costs above Rs.5,000/- will be referred to banks concerned by the District B.C. Service Cooperative Societies.

All cases with unit costs of less than Rs.5,000/- will be handled by the District B.C. Service Cooperative Societies themselves.

The Cases referred to banks will be grounded following the same procedure as is being followed for I.R.D.P. schemes grounded with bank loan.

Grounding of Group Activities

Units may be grounded for groups of beneficiaries following C.M.E.Y. or DWACRA pattern. The number of beneficiaries could be increased depending upon the activity and tools to be used. A power operated wool shearing machine can for example cater to the shearing needs of a large number of shepherds.

Grounding of group units could be done in two ways. Especially in trades like Carpentry where some of the power tools are complementary in nature, one type of tool can be owned by one member and the members can pool their tools and come together as a group for working. In cases like goldsmithy where the cost of the equipment itself is high, the groups may be formed prior to purchase of tools/ equipment in favour of the group to facilitate grounding with higher investments.

Care may be taken to ensure that the groups are compact and functional.

Procurement of Tools

Once the selection of tools is finalised by the beneficiaries, the District B.C. Service Cooperative Societies will consolidate the requirements and place orders with the manufacturer/supplier firms concerned.

The manufacturers/suppliers while supplying the tools will raise the invoice in the name of District B.C. Service Cooperative Society concerned and deliver the tools equipment at Mandal Headquarters to the M.D.O.

The prices of various tools to be procured from the identified manufacturers dealers will be determined by a committee comprising some District Collectors, that is to be constituted exclusively for this purpose. The prices so determined will be uniformly applicable for the specific tools to be supplied under the project throughout the State.

In addition, if tools, other than those finalized by the above committee, are to be procured from the local firms, within the district it should be done as per the approval of the District Collector concerned.

The existing distribution channels of the manufacturers/suppliers concerned will be utilised to ensure effective supply of tools equipment at the mandal level.

All tools supplied under the project will be inspected, before distribution to the beneficiaries, and their quality is to be certified by a Committee of Experts, to be constituted by the District Collectors.

Payments as indicated by Head Office will be made through the District B.C. Service Cooperative Society in certain percentages (guidelines in this regard will be intimated by Head Office), after the equipment is received by the Mandal Development Officer after the inspection team certifies the quality and after delivery of the tools/ equipment to the beneficiary.

All manufacturers suppliers of tools under the project shall extend unconditional performance guarantee for their tools at least for one year, during which period the defective tools should be replaced by new tools of same specifications as the ones supplied earlier. Arrangements are being made by Head Office to enter into legal agreements with suppliers in this regard.

All tools and the life of the beneficiary will be insured for the period of loan. Arrangements are being made by Head Office to tie-up with Insurance Companies in this regard.

Distribution of Assets

Assets will be distributed to the beneficiaries in asset distribution functions to be organised at Mandal headquarters or at other places on a monthly basis.

Organisational Support

Additional manpower, at all levels will be augmented for the effective and timely implementation of the project. District Collectors are empowered to take on deputation, additional officers of the rank of Deputy Tehsildars or above from any Department—one each for a Revenue Division and one for district office—to work exclusively on the project.

One Data Entry Operator could also be engaged at the district level on deputation basis to assist the Executive Director, B.C. Service Cooperative Society in computerisation of the project related data and information.

National Institute of Information Technology will extend customised application of software and technical support, to the Head Office and District B.C. Service Cooperative Societies, on a continual basis, for the creation and maintenance of relevant data for the project. For the purpose, all District B.C. Service Cooperative Societies will be provided with necessary computer hardware, software and Internet facility.

Overall Supervision and Monitoring

Implementation of **ADARANA** at the district level will be monitored by the Minister incharge of DDRC.

The programme will be implemented entirely by the District Collectors. District Collectors may co-opt other District Officers in addition to the Executive Directors of B.C. Service Cooperative Society for the effective implementation of the project in the district.

District Collectors are requested to form a Tools Purchasing Committee at the district level with Collector as Chairperson, another senior officer of his choice as a Member and the Executive Director of District B.C. Service Cooperative Society as Member Convenor, for making purchases under the project and also for supervising the project implementation.

Marketing

Marketing is an entrepreneurial function, Marketing net work in several cases is more expensive than the production outfit. Quite often artisan units find it difficult to produce quality goods at economic costs. Artisan units can expand production and improve quality with technical assistance and financial support from the large marketing companies. There is vast scope for promoting such marketing companies. India has a natural advantage in exports of such items where labour inputs are considerable like gem and jewellery, garments, carpets, leather, footwear uppers, footwear, leather goods, silk, handlooms, handicrafts etc. The export efforts are assisted by several export promotion councils industry-wise like Apparel, Handlooms, Handicrafts Gem and Jewellery, Leather, Silk etc. For internal marketing there are a large number of State Corporations, Cooperative Societies, Apex Cooperative Societies and emporia and sales outlets of various organisations. At the centre also there are marketing outlets like Central Cottage Industries Emporium, sales outlets of Khadi and Village Industries Commission and Coir Board. Rural markets is one of the areas which has not received significant attention. Opening of sales outlets in rural areas are to be picked up, since it is costly in towns.

Artisan Status in the District

The important artisan trades that are existing in Kurnool district are blacksmithy, carpentry, bamboo basket making, cobblery, pottery, stone cutting stone carving etc. Carpentry, blacksmithy, pottery and cobblery are covered in almost all the mandals. Bamboo basket manufacturing is found mainly in Atmakur, Srisailam, Kothapalli, Velugodu, Rudravaram, Siruvella, Chagalamarri, Adoni, Pathikonda, Gonegandla and Peapully Mandals. Mat weaving is found mainly in Banaganapalli, Chagalamarri and Atmakur Mandals. Rope making can be found mainly in Jupadu Bungalow, Dornipadu, Koilakuntla, Sanjamala, Bandi-Atmakur, Banaganapalli and Mantralayam Mandals. Broom making is found in Rudravaram, Maddikera, Tuggali and Devanakonda Mandals. Lime burning is found mainly in Banaganapalli, Rudravaram, Chagalamarri, Kolimigundla, Koilakuntla and Sanjamala Mandals. Stone carving is found in Allagadda, Gadivemula, Holagunda and Krishnagiri mandals. Stone cutting is mainly found in Kolimigundla, and Owk Mandals.

After Independence, the Government have been making concerted efforts to encourage the revival of the cottage industries through financial assistance and providing training facilities to the artisans. The Industries Department implemented a number of schemes in the district for training the artisans in rural arts, crafts and industries. The District Industries Centre has also implemented artisan complexes in the district in different trades. It has supplied tool kits to the artisans. The Khadi and Village Industries Board is providing financial assistance for the activities coming under its purview. The amount of assistance differs from industry to industry from one scheme to another for each industry. The District Rural Development Agency is giving subsidies to the artisans under I.R.D.P. programme and also arranging training to the needed artisans. The A.P.S.F.C. Kurnool Branch and Commercial Banks are assisting the artisans by providing finance for setting up their new artisan complexes and industrial cooperative societies.

Artisan Complexes

This programme is similar to that of industrial estates Industrial accommodation is provided to the artisans by bringing their activity outside their residential localities. In these complexes house-cum-worksheds will be provided besides providing financial assistance by the financial agencies to meet their working capital requirements and equipment cost. Under this programme as many as 83 artisan complexes in different trades like pottery, slab polishing, carpentry, blacksmithy, handloom weaving, rope making, broom sticks, thunga mat weaving etc. were taken up. These complexes were established with an investment of

Rs.178.29 Lakhs providing employment to 2316 artisans. Out of these 83 complexes 17 are of slab polishing, 12 are of pottery, 8 are of rope making, 7 are of carpentry, 2 are of carpentery and blacksmith complexes and 3 are basket making complexes and remaining are of miscellaneous nature.

Artisan Survey Conducted

The District Industries Centre has conducted an artisan survey in the district and identified 17,883 artisans. These do not include trades like tailoring, handloom weaving, cumbly weaving. The trade wise particulars of these artisans are given in Annexure-I. The mandal wise particulars are tabulated in Annexure-II at the end of this chapter. The purpose of the artisan survey conducted by the District Industries Centre is to provide improved tool kits through I.R.D.P. Programme by D.R.D.A. to the artisans who cannot afford improved tools on their own. The artisans like carpenters, blacksmiths, leather workers, stone carvers potters, bamboo basket makers etc. are confined to rural areas and utilising the locally available raw materials and use their traditional tools. The articles produced by these artisans are mostly against orders given by local people thereby. Their activity is thus confined to the time of getting the work from the villagers.

Hence the earning capacity of any category of artisans is highly restricted and they are highly dependent upon other activities for sustenance like agricultural labour, quarrying and miscellaneous jobs. In addition to the above, with the usage of age old traditional tools the quality of the product is poor and the drudgery is more. Since the quality of the goods produced is inferior, the prices that they command is very low, the economic conditions of the artisan is deteriorating year by year and he is unable to continue in his present vocation and develop his skills. It is with this objective that this proposal to give assistance to this category of population is conceived and proposed. In the absence of this relief, the artisan is compelled either to abandon his skill or to migrate to urban areas to eke out his livelihood. This situation can be arrested by taking advantage of the infrastructure developments that have taken place in the villages like electrification, development of improved tools, upgradation of skills and the economic conditions of the artisans can be improved to a degree of economic self sufficiency. Out of the total 17,883 artisan population, 9176 artisans are already covered by different programmes wherein services for extending tool kits and other inputs like working capital etc. were provided through D.R.D.A. and District Industries Centre, still leaving a balance of 8,707 artisans who need to be assisted at present. Out of these artisan populations, 7,580 are stone cutters, who are actually working in quarries like granites, napa slabs, lime stone mines etc., and 80 per cent of these workers i.e., 6064 artisans have the required hand tools. Hence assistance is to be provided at present to the remaining 20 per cent stone cutters i.e., 1516 stone cutters inclusive of the remaining different categories of artisans, the total unassisted artisans will be 2643. Time relief was given to them also.

Raw Materials

The main trades to be assisted are carpentry, blacksmithy, pottery, basket making, stone carvers, broom stick making, leather tanning, cobblery, lime burning, stone cutter etc. for which raw materials are abundantly available locally without much difficulty.

Upgradation of Skills

Some of the artisans require a short term training in the usage of improved hand tools and in the upgradation of skills, enabling them to use modern trends effectively. This short term training would be taken up under TRYSEM Programme of the D.R.D.A.

Provision of Improved Tool Kits

After upgrading the skills wherever required, modern tools are to be supplied to these artisans so that the quality of goods produced would be upto the taste of urban population and the goods so produced will find ready market in urban centres. At present an average artisan, using traditional tools and low quality articles is able to earn Rs.10/- to 15/- a day. By upgrading the skills and by introducing improved tools, the quality of the product will also be improved, and simultaneously fetch higher rate of returns to the artisans.

Total Outlay

The number of artisans tradewise who require to be provided with financial assistance is given in Annexure-III at the end of this chapter. As seen from the Annexure, 10 trade activities are proposed to be covered under this programme of financial assistance. The details of tools to be provided in each trade is given in Annexure-IV at the end of this chapter. The total outlay required for the project is Rs.40.60 lakhs, out of which the artisans contribution is 10 per cent i.e., Rs. 4.06 lakhs. The government of India's assistance required is to the extent of Rs. 36.54 lakhs. With this assistance from the Government, 2643 families will be benefited directly by getting their economic status improved.

ANNEXURE—I

Sl. No.	Name of the Trade	No. of Artisans Identified	No. of Artisans already provided assistance through DRDA/D.I.C.	No. of Artisans who have improved tool kits with them on their own	No. of Artisans requiring assistance	No. of Artisans which can be provided assistance	Remarks
1.	Blacksmithy	1247	1120	–	127	127	The figure shown in Col. 5 relate to only improved tool kit i.e., at present all of these have traditional tool kits and its proposed to provide them improved tool kits for skill upgradation and increase income.
2.	Carpentry	2137	1877	–	260	560	
3.	Bamboo Basket	2285	1999	–	286	286	
4.	Broom Making	179	150	–	29	29	
5.	Cobblery	1771	1690	–	162	162	
6.	Leather Tanning	63	63	–	–	–	
7.	Pottery	1216	1094	–	122	122	
8.	Stone Carving	98	33	–	65	65	
9.	Rope Making	224	224	–	–	–	
10.	Brick making	468	468	–	–	–	
11.	Mat weaving	236	236	–	–	–	
12.	Lime Burning	309	242	–	67	67	
13.	Adda Leaf	60	60	–	–	–	
14.	Goldsmith	9	–	–	9	9	
15.	Kalankari	1	1	–	–	–	
16.	Stone Cutting	7580	–	6064	1516	1516	
		17883	9176	6064	2643	2643	

ANNEXURE—II

Abstract of Artisans Identified in Nandyal Parliamentary Constituency Mandal-size

Sl. No.	*Name of the Mandal*	*Carp entry*	*Bamboo Basket*	*Black-smithy*	*Pottery*	*Cobblery*	*Mat Weaving*	*Rope Making*	*Broom Making*	*Lime Burning*	*Stone Carving*	*Stone Cutting*	*Adda leaf*	*Leather tenning*	*Brick making*
1.	Atmakur and Srisailam	96	540	22	62	71	20	–	–	–	–	–	–	–	20
2.	Kothapalli	61	100	34	16	36	–	–	–	–	–	–	–	–	–
3.	Pamulapadu	52	60	21	2	38	10	–	–	–	–	15	–	–	–
4.	Velugodu	81	150	29	30	10	–	–	–	–	–	91	60	–	–
5.	Japadu Bungalow	23	22	11	30	2	–	20	–	–	–	–	–	–	–
6.	Pagidyala	26	–	24	7	16	–	–	–	–	–	–	–	–	–
7.	Midthur	34	4	17	22	–	–	–	–	–	–	–	–	–	–
8.	Nandikotkur	47	40	14	12	30	–	–	–	–	–	–	–	–	–
9.	Allagadda	92	73	33	36	66	–	–	–	–	40	–	–	–	–
10.	Chagalamarri	74	83	26	48	88	20	–	–	20	–	–	–	–	–
11.	Gospadu	21	2	12	–	21	4	–	–	–	–	–	–	–	–
12.	Rudravaram	107	99	88	93	99	5	–	65	90	–	–	–	–	20
13.	Sirvel	130	100	72	50	33	10	–	–	–	–	–	–	–	20
14.	Kolimigundla	27	–	8	28	30	–	–	–	20	–	3950	–	20	–
15.	Dornipadu	8	–	5	–	–	–	25	–	–	–	–	–	–	–
16.	Koilakuntla	21	60	6	30	66	–	20	–	23	–	300	–	–	–

(Contd...)

Sl. No.	Name of the Mandal	Carp-entry	Bamboo Basket	Black-smithy	Pottery	Cobblery	Mat Weaving	Rope Making	Broom Making	Lime Burning	Stone Carving	Stone Cutting	Adda leaf	Leather tenning	Brick making
17.	Uyyalawada	49	–	6	27	59	–	2	–	–	–	60	–	–	–
18.	Sanjamala	32	5	5	45	76	2	25	–	28	–	90	–	–	–
19.	Gadivemula	32	–	–	3	24	–	–	–	–	23	–	–	–	–
20.	Mahanandi	30	250	2	–	8	–	–	–	–	–	–	–	–	135
21.	Panyam	35	–	18	37	31	–	–	–	–	–	–	–	–	20
22.	Bandi-Atmakur	69	96	19	21	12	10	30	–	–	–	–	–	–	–
23.	Nandyal	34	–	5	10	36	–	–	–	–	–	–	–	–	–
24.	Banaganapalli	104	5	54	31	194	130	18	–	104	–	355	–	–	–
25.	Owk	37	9	20	9	50	10	–	–	–	–	2084	–	–	–
26.	Bethamcherla	41	17	20	68	19	10	–	–	–	–	50	–	–	–
27.	Veldurthy	48	23	38	10	25	–	–	–	–	–	26	–	–	–
28.	Orvakal	59	–	49	50	32	10	–	–	–	–	50	–	20	–
	Total	1460	1763	675	864	1172	23	140	–	285	63	7071	–	20	465

Total 14, 334

Abstract of Artisans of Kurnool Parliamentary Constituency—Mandal-size

Sl. No.	Name of the Mandal	Carp-entry	Bamboo Basket	Black-smithy	Pottery	Cobblery	Mat Weaving	Rope Making	Broom Making	Lime Burning	Stone Carving	Stone Cutting	Adda leaf	Leather tenning	Brick making	Kalam Kari	Gold-smith
1.	Yemmlganur	43	18	17	19	11	–	12	–	–	57	–	–	5	–	–	1
2.	C. Belagal	28	–	45	–	26	–	–	–	–	–	–	–	–	–	–	3
3.	Kosigi	62	9	9	40	57	–	–	–	3	1	–	–	17	–	–	–
4.	Adoni	76	68	49	11	38	3	–	–	2	37	–	–	1	2	–	–
5.	Dhone	3	42	15	–	2	–	–	–	–	1	–	–	–	–	–	–
6.	Pathikonda	56	52	–	36	12	–	–	–	–	–	–	–	–	–	–	–
7.	Mantralayam	17	–	2	1	10	–	38	6	–	–	–	–	–	–	–	–
8.	Nandavaram	20	–	18	37	10	–	1	–	2	3	–	–	4	–	–	–
9.	Kurnool (Other than Municipality)	31	5	53	5	21	–	–	8	–	–	–	–	7	–	–	–
10.	Kodumur	2	4	33	–	8	–	1	–	–	–	–	–	–	–	1	1
11.	Gudur	3	11	10	53	2	–	–	1	–	–	–	–	8	–	–	–
12.	Pedda Kodbur	27	5	32	7	19	–	–	2	3	–	–	–	1	–	–	–
13.	Kowthalam	32	–	15	6	28	–	4	–	–	–	–	–	–	–	–	–
14.	Maddikera	8	–	14	–	2	–	–	24	–	–	–	–	–	–	–	–

Sl. No.	Name of the Mandal	Carpentry	Bamboo Basket	Blacksmithy	Pottery	Cobblery	Mat Weaving	Rope Making	Broom Making	Lime Burning	Stone Carving	Stone Cutting	Adda leaf	Leather tenning	Brick making	Kalam Kari	Goldsmith
15.	Tuggali	17	–	28	9	14	–	1	30	–	–	3	–	–	–	–	–
16.	Devanakonda	17	–	16	1	2	–	–	28	–	–	–	–	–	–	–	–
17.	Gonegandla	10	55	35	5	8	–	–	–	–	–	–	–	–	–	–	–
18.	Kallur	29	28	50	12	73	–	5	15	–	–	–	–	–	–	–	–
19.	Hoagunda	40	47	4	23	32	–	–	–	–	10	19	–	–	–	–	–
20.	Chippagiri	41	18	11	4	20	–	11	–	–	83	4	–	–	–	–	–
21.	Ajur	49	43	30	33	50	–	1	–	–	206	–	–	–	–	–	–
22.	Aspari	23	–	17	1	24	–	2	–	9	47	–	–	–	–	–	–
23.	Peapully	15	55	29	9	11	–	3	–	5	13	–	–	–	1	–	–
24.	Krishnagiri	6	17	33	4	6	–	5	–	–	–	9	–	–	–	–	–
25.	Halaharvi	20	45	24	26	113	2	–	–	–	52	–	–	–	–	–	4
	Total	677	522	572	352	599	5	84	114	24	509	35	–	43	3	1	9

Total Artisans: 3549

ANNEXURE—III

Financial Assistance of Rural Artisans

Sl. No.	Name of the Trade	Number of artisans who get assistance	Unit Cost Rs.	Amount spent (Rs. in Lakhs)	Govt. of India Contribution 90%	Artisan Contribution 10%
1.	Blacksmithy	127	6000	7.620	6.858	0.762
2.	Carpentry	260	3000	7.800	7.020	0.780
3.	Bamboo Basket Making	286	500	1.430	1.287	0.143
4.	Broom Making	29	500	0.145	0.130	0.015
5.	Cobblery	162	1000	1.620	1.458	0.162
6.	Pottery	122	3000	3.660	3.294	0.366
7.	Stone Carving	65	1500	0.975	0.878	0.097
8.	Lime Burning	67	3000	2.010	1.809	0.201
9.	Goldsmithy	9	2000	0.180	0.162	0.018
10.	Stone Cutting	1516	1000	15.160	13.644	1.516
	Total	2643		40.600	36.54	4.06

ANNEXURE—IV

Improved Toolkits for the Artisans

Sl.No.	Name of the Trade		Name of the improved toolkits				Number
1.	Carpentry	1.	Raily's wolf hand drilling machine				1 No.
		2.	Shash Bar Gram		6 Ft		2 Nos.
		3.	Half round wood rough files				
			10 Inches	–	Rough		1 No.
					–	Smooth	1 No.
		4.	Round files	–	Rough		1 No.
		5.	G. Clamps	–	–	Smooth	1 No.
					8 inches		4 Nos.
						6 Inches	4 Nos.
		6.	Chisels 1/4" to 2"				1 Set
		7.	Augers 1/8" to 4/3"				1 Set
		8.	Planes				2 Nos.
		9.	Bench vice				2 Nos.
		10.	Trysquare				1 No.
		11.	Footrules	–	Wooden		2 Nos.
					–	Steel	2 Nos.
		12.	Cutting Pliers				2 Nos.
		13.	Pincers				2 Nos.
		14.	Hand Saw	–	2 Ft		1 No.
		15.	Tenosaw		–	1/4	1 No.
		16.	Fret Saw				1 No.

Sl.No.	Name of the Trade		Name of the improved toolkits	Number
2.	Blacksmithy	1.	Blower (18" with 1/2 HP Motor)	1 No.
		2.	Sewage Block – 1 Cwt.	1 No.
		3.	Sludge Hammer	1 No.
		4.	Anvil with steel top – 1 Cvt.	1 No.
		5.	Double Heanded Hand Hammers – 1 Cwt.	2 Nos.
		6.	Tonges	1 No.
		7.	Leg Vice 4"	1 No.
		8.	Hot Chisels	1 No.
		9.	Spanner Set	1 Set
3.	Pottery	1.	Improved ball-bearing Pottery wheel devised by Rajiv Technology Mission.	1 No.
		2.	Wheel Barrow	
		3.	Hand tools	1 No.
4.	Stone Carving		Improved tools developed by all India Handicrafts Board	
5.	Stone Cutting		Chisels, Crowbars, hammers, Spades, Gamalas, Headgear	
6.	Bamboo Basket		Tools designed by All India Handicrafts Board.	
7.	Brooms		Knives, Metal Brush	
8.	Cobblery		Cutting Knives, Rampieces, Irontryleg, Hammer, Cutting Plier, Pincer, Oil Stone, Eye letting set, Brushes.	
9.	Glodsmsithy		Blow lamp, Small anvil, Hammers set, Nose pliers, Blower, Foreceps, Moulds, Balance and Weights.	
10.	Lime Burners		Improved Bhatti, Crowbars, Gamalas, Spades, Iron rod.	

5

Socio-Economic Conditions of Artisans in Kurnool District

A detailed survey has been conducted by taking samples in five trades such as carpentry, bamboo basket making, blacksmithy, goldsmithy and cobblery. The earlier two trades are found in Atmakur, and Velugodu Revenue Mandals. The Nallamalla Forest has become a source for the supply of raw materials such as wood of various kinds and bamboos. The artisans of these trades are personally contacted and details obtained. In case of blacksmithy and goldsmithy, survey has been taken up in Nandyal and Adoni Revenue Mandals. These artisans also are contacted for relevant information. In fact, the study is confined to cluster villages to make the research project comprehensive enough. Five trades comprising 100 artisans are subjected to close study.

Trade Wise Distribution of Artisans-Statistical Data

Out of 100 artisans in all, 20 belong to carpentry 20 to blacksmithy; 20 to cobblery; 20 were bamboo basket makers, and 20 to goldsmithy. As it is already pointed out majority of carpenters belong to Atmakur Revenue Mandal and majority of bamboo basket makers to Velugodu Revenue Mandal. Table 5.1 overleaf shows the Mandal wise and activity wise data of these artisans.

Age Group

Majority of these artisans belong to the age group of 40 years and above. Only 7 artisans belonging to cobblery, carpentry and goldsmithy are of the age between 18 and 24 years. It is significant to note, none of the blacksmithy, bamboo basket making is below 25 years. For uniformity the artisans are selected from the age group between 18 and 40 years. It is gathered from the survey that artisans of 40 years and above have given sufficient and useful information for this survey.

Literacy

It is particularly observed that most of the artisans are illiterate. Out of these 100 artisans only 15 attended school education. The others had no school education and some of them said that they had undergone formal training in their trade. Table 5.2 shows that about 45 per cent had some formal education, 7 per cent primary, 8 per cent secondary education, 40% have neither primary nor secondary, nor even formal education, and hence 15 per cent are literates, whereas 85 per cent (45 per cent formal education + 40 per cent totally illiterates) are illiterates. It is also observed that literacy rate in Kurnool rural areas is very low.

Skill

Almost all these artisans are traditionally trained in their respective trade. Only one artisan in carpentery and another in blacksmithy are reported to have institutional training. All these artisans have got traditional competency.

Tradition and Duration of Stay

100 artisans connected with goldsmithy, carpentry, blacksmithy, cobblery, and bamboo basket making are taken up for survey. Out of 100 samples in all, 75 artisans have inherited their occupation and skill from the elder members in the family and with regard to the period of their stay in the tradition it has been noted 46 per cent have been engaged in their respective trade for over 16 years. Some of them have been working for over 30 years. There are only 3 artisans who have been working for less than 5 years in their trade. 19 artisans have been working for 6 to 10 years; 32 for over 10 years, but less than 15 years. To sum up 95 per cent

Table 5.1: Trade-wise Distribution of Sample Artisans in Study Area

Sl.No.	*Type of Artisan*	*Atmakur*	*Velugodu*	*Nandyal*	*Adoni*	*Dhone*	*Kurnool*	*Nandikotkur*	*Yemmiganur*	*Gudur*	*C. Belagal*	*Total*
1.	Carpentry	8	2	2	–	–	3	3	2	–	–	20
2.	Blacksmithy	2	3	1	2	3	2	2	–	3	2	20
3.	Cobblery	1	1	3	3	4	2	1	2	2	1	20
4.	Bamboo Basket	2	8	1	2	2	1	1	1	–	2	20
5.	Glodsmith	–	–	5	6	2	4	2	1	–	–	20
	Total	13	14	12	13	11	12	9	6	5	5	100

Source: Field Survey.

From the selected 10 mandals a total of 100 respondents were contacted and elicited the information from the concerning five rural artisan trades selected for the survey.

Table 5.2: Trade-wise Distribution of Artisans by Age, Literacy and Level of Training

Sl.No.	*Trade*	*Age Group*			*Level of literacy*				*Level of training*			*No. of Artisans in each trade*
		18-24	*25-40*	*40 +*	*Formal*	*Primary*	*Secondary*	*Illiterate*	*Technical*	*Formal*	*Traditional*	
1.	Carpentry	1	3	16	9(45%)	2(10%)	3(15%)	6(30%)	1	–	19	20
2.	Blacksmithy	–	–	20	11(55%)	2(10%)	2(10%)	5(25%)	1	–	19	20
3.	Cobblery	5	6	9	7(35%)	1(5%)	1(5%)	11(55%)	–	–	20	20
4.	Bamboo Basket Making	–	2	18	4(20%)	–	–	16(80%)	–	–	20	20
5.	Glodsmith	7	3	16	14(70%)	2(10%)	2(10%)	2(10%)	–	–	20	20
	Total	7	14	79	45	7	8	40	2	–	98	100

Source: Field Survey.

artisans have been engaged in their present trade for over 10 years. It is significant to note that almost all these artisans entered their trade while they were quite young.

Blacksmiths entered their trade around 15 years ago. In case of carpenters and bamboo basket makers it is partly true. Cobblers and goldsmiths, almost all have stayed in their trades quite some time now. From the above analysis we come to know that the fact that 46 per cent of the artisans working for over 16 years in their respective trades show that they have no adequate alternative source of employment in rural areas. Another inference from this analysis is that these artisans stick on to their trades with strong will, persistence and perseverance. All these artisans entered their trades traditionally on caste basis, Table 5.3 depicts the distribution of artisans by year of stay in the inherited trade/in the trade started by the present generation.

Main and Subsidiary Occupation of the Rural Artisans

It is noticeable that 77 per cent of the artisans are engaged in their present trade as their main occupation. The remaining 23 per cent take to their trade to eke out their livelihood as their subsidiary occupation, while their main occupation is agriculture. A few artisans of goldsmithy who live in the urban area take their trade as their main occupation while those who live in the rural areas take to agriculture as their main occupation. These goldsmiths of the villages get meagre income by this trade. On the whole, 77 per cent artisans depend mainly on their trade for their livelihood while 23 per cent get meagre income from this trade. Their major source of income happens to be cultivation. Table 5.4 depicts trade distribution of Artisans by Main/Subsidiary occupation.

Annual Income of the Artisans

The annual Income of artisans belonging to these five trades is surveyed and analysed and can be broadly into two categories. In the first category goldsmiths, carpenters and blacksmiths can be mentioned. They belong to high income

Table 5.3: Distribution of Artisans by Years of Stay in the Trade Inherited/started by Present Generation

Sl.No.	*Trade*	*Inherited (Years)*				*Started by present generation*				*No. of artisans is each grade*
		0-5	*6-10*	*11-15*	*16 +*	*0-5*	*6-10*	*11-15*	*16 +*	
1.	Carpentry	–	4	5	2	–	5	4	–	20
2.	Blacksmithy	–	–	4	15	—	–	–	1	20
3.	Cobblery	3	8	5	–	–	1	2	1	20
4.	Bamboo Basket Making	–	–	1	18	–	1	–	–	20
5.	Glodsmith	–	–	5	5	–	–	6	4	20
	Total	3	12	20	40 (75%)	–	7	12	6	100

Source: Field Survey.

Table 5.4: Trade Wise Distribution of Artisans by Main/Subsidiary Occupation

Sl. No.	*Trade*	*No. of Artisans*	*Main Occupation*	*Subsidiary Occupation*	*% of Main Occupation*	*% Subsidiary Occcupation*
1.	Carpentry	20	11	9	55	45
2.	Blacksmithy	20	18	2	90	10
3.	Cobblery	20	11	9	55	45
4.	Bamboo Basket Making	20	17	3	85	45
5.	Goldsmithy	20	20	–	100	–

Source: **Field Survey.**

group among artisans. Their annual income ranges from Rs. 3000/- to Rs. 30,000/-. The Income of the goldsmith is the highest. It is so because most of the goldsmiths work in urban areas and are already financially sound. They come under affluent category. It is also because the investment is bound to be very high; in this respect next comes carpentry, this trade is found equally in urban and rural areas. These artisans work in rural areas supply their products to the customers belonging to urban areas, of course, some of them cater to the needs of village community hence their income can be placed next to the goldsmith in the gradation. In case of blacksmithy the requirement for it is more in the rural areas than in the urban areas. Thus the major source of income happens to be rural customers. Evidently the income of this category occupies third place in the gradation. The other two kinds of artisans belonging to cobblery, and bamboo basket making come under low income group. Their annual income does not exceed Rs. 3000/-. Cobblers mainly work in rural areas and rarely work in urban areas. In either case their income is always small. Bamboo basket makers work in rural areas and supply their product to the wholesalers in urban areas. Very few of these artisans take up retail sales. In either case their income is the least in the gradation. The following Table 5.5 is self explanatory in this respect.

Table 5.5: Annual Income of the Rural Artisans—Kurnool District

Sl. No.	*Type of Artisan Activity*	*Annual Income*	
		Per Artisan Family	*Per Artisan Earner*
1.	Carpentry	6002.73	3159.47
2.	Blacksmithy	1743.75	1395.00
3.	Cobblery	1262.50	1262.50
4.	Bamboo Basket Making	1395.71	476.59
5.	Glodsmith	10294.00	4541.47

Source: Field Survey.

Per Capita Income of Artisan Earner/Artisan Family

In this analysis the inference is in accordance with the annual income as shown in the subheading mentioned above. A goldsmith occupies the first place among these five trades so far as individual and family incomes are concerned. The artisans belonging to carpentry earn individually about half of the income of the family as a group, on the other hand, family earning of a blacksmith is nearly equal to that of his fmaily. But in case of cobblery the income of an artisan is less than that of his family. The earnings of bamboo basket makers is in the reverse order, i.e., the income of an artisan is more than that of his family in the bamboo basket making trade. To overcome the difficulty of making both ends meet the involvement of the members of the family in respect of bamboo basket makers is more. Thus they partly solve the problem of their livelihood Table 5.6 interpret the ranks on the basis of Annual Incomes of different trades.

Table 5.6: Ranks on the Basis of Annual Incomes—Kurnool District

Sl. No.	*Artisan Trade*	*Ranks on the basis of the Family Income*	*Rank on the basis of the Income per earner*
1.	Goldsmith	1	1
2.	Carpentry	2	2
3.	Blacksmithy	3	3
4.	Cobblery	5	4
5.	Bamboo Basket Making	4	5

Source: Field Survey.

Extent of Employment in Different Trades

Most of these artisans are not engaged in their trade throughout the year. Even if some artisans belonging to carpentry and bamboo basket making work throughout the year their income varies from time to time depending upon the monsoon and agriculture yields. These artisans work at the most for about 200 days a year. However their working days range from 150 to 200. Around 40 per cent of the artisans are reported to have work for 150 to 200 days in a year. 70 per cent of the blacksmiths 50 per cent of carpenters and 40 per cent of bamboo basket makers come under this group. Around 25 per cent of artisans in all do not work for even 150 days a year. However all these artisans on an average around 36.1 per cent, of work for over 200 days. The overall picture shows that around 75 per cent of these artisans are engaged in their trade for a minimum period in a year Table 5.7 shows the extent of employment in different trades.

Table 5.7: Extent of Employment in Different Trades

Sl. No.	*Trade*	*No. of Artisans*	*Extent of Employment*		
			Less than 150 Days	*150-200 Days*	*200 +*
1.	Carpentry	20	2(10%)	10(50%)	8(40%)
2.	Blacksmithy	20	2(10%)	14(70%)	4(20%)
3.	Cobblery	20	3(15%)	2(10%)	15(75%)
4.	Bamboo Basket Making	20	7(35%)	8(40%)	5(25%)
5.	Goldsmith	20	11(55%)	5(25%)	4(20%)
	All trades	100	25	39	36

Source: Personal observation.

Extent of Family Labour/Hired Labour

In almost all these trades the head of the family and even some members of the family work in their trades. In respect of bamboo basket makers almost all the members of the family are engaged in this trade. Around 1/3 of all these artisans are skilled and the rest are unskilled. In respect of bamboo basket makers cobblery and blacksmith majority members of each family are engaged in these trades. However, hired labour is also employed. The ratio between the owner labour and hired labour is about 3:1. 20 per cent of hired labour in cobblery and blacksmithy is employed. The hired labour in bamboo basket making is comparatively very small. Skilled workers are hired in many cases. Around 75 per cent of hired labour is skilled and the rest unskilled. Women and children of a family are employed as unskilled labour. In case of goldsmithy, there are apprentices goldsmiths employed on wages. Some master goldsmith are not by themselves skilled workers neither are the members of their family. Majority of hired labour in this respect is skilled. The woman member participation in trades like carpentry, blacksmith, cobblery and goldsmithy is either nil or insignificant. As a matter of fact, goldsmithy and carpentry require highly skilled labour, whereas blacksmithy and cobblery require less skilled labour and bamboo basket making requires least amount of skilled labour. Therefore the involvement of members of the family in respect of bamboo basket making is maximum Table 5.8 describes the Extent of family, labour and hired, labour in different trades.

Table 5.8: Extent of Family Labour and Hired Labour in Different Trade

Sl. No.	*Trade*	*Units*	*Family Labour*		*Hired Labour*		*Total*
			Skilled	*Unskilled*	*Skilled*	*Unskilled*	
1.	Carpentry	20	19 (52.77%)	6 (16.66%)	7 (19.44%)	4 (11.11%)	36
2.	Blacksmithy	20	25 (64.10%)	8 (20.51%)	2 (5.12%)	4 (10.25%)	39
3.	Cobblery	20	24 (66.66%)	4. (11.11%)	6 (16.66%)	2 (5.55%)	36
4.	Bamboo Basket Making	20	52 (78.78%)	12 (18.18%)	1 (1.51%)	1 (1.51%)	66
5.	Goldsmithy	20	25 (45.01%)	13 (25.49%)	10 (19.60%)	3 (5.88%)	51
	All trades	20	145	43	26	14	228

Source: Field Survey.

Trade Wise Distribution of Male/Female and Children

Men artisans form, more than 70 per cent of the total labour. In case of hired labour only men are employed. Women labour is of minor importance. It is mainly found in bamboo basket making. The employment of child labour in all the five trades is very meagre. Men labourers play a major role in carpentry, blacksmithy and cobblery. Mostly men are hired in goldsmithy and carpentry. Women labour is almost nil in respect of blacksmithy. The ratio of hired labour to total family labour is vary about 25 per cent Table 5.9 depicts the trade wise distribution of Male/Female and Child labour.

Wages of Hired Labour

The wage rates of goldsmithy, carpentry, blacksmithy, cobblery and bamboo basket making are descending in the order of the trades mentioned. Goldsmithy and carpentry require technically qualified or skilled worker, and hence these artisans are generally employed on monthly wages. Artisans of carpentry get Rs. 1500/- per month, while those of goldsmithy and blacksmithy get Rs. 1200/- and 800/- respectively. Bamboo basket makers get monthly emoluments of Rs. 700/- only. Children are employed only in goldsmithy and are paid Rs. 300/- each per month. Women artisans in blacksmithy get Rs. 600/- each per month. The overall impression is that artisans in carpentry and goldsmithy get very small wages. Moreover, women artisans are discriminated by smaller wages. Table 5.10 explain wages of hired labour.

Production and its Value

The finished products from all the five trades are only traditional items catering to the local needs. Carpenters for example make house hold furniture like chairs, tables, carts and almirahs, wooden fixtures and farm tools like ploughs and carts. Some of them make and repair only agricultural implements. Very few carpenters supply their product to the urban areas. Most of the carpenters live in Atmakur Revenue Mandal.

Blacksmith also make agricultural implements such as ploughs, crow bars, buckets, axes and pick-axes and ox-shoes. These are common tools found in villages. Ambidexterous, some practice both carpentry and blacksmithy and make all these agricultural implements and also undertake repairs.

Table 5.9: Trade-wise Distribution of Male/Female/Child Labour

Sl. No.	Trade	*Family Labour*			*Hired Labour*			*Total Labour*		
		Male	*Female*	*Children*	*Male*	*Female*	*Children*	*Male*	*Female*	*Children*
1.	Carpentry	25 (69.44)	–	–	11 (30.56)	–	–	36	–	–
2.	Blacksmithy	28 (77.77)	2 (75.00)	–	8 (22.23)	1 (25.00)	–	36	3	–
3.	Cobblery	26 (76.47)	–	2 (100.00)	8 (23.53)	–	–	34	–	2
4.	Bamboo Basket Making	52 (96.29)	8 (100)	4 (100.00)	2 (3.71)	–	–	54	8	4
5.	Goldsmithy	36 (81.81)	–	2 (75.00)	8 (18.18)	–	1 (25.00)	44	–	3
	All Trades	167 (74.55)	10 (4.46)	8 (3.57)	37 (16.5)	1 (0.44)	1 (0.44)	204	11	9

Source: Field Survey.

Table 5.10: Wages of Hired Labour

(per month per artisan)

Sl. No.	*Type of Artisan Activity*	*Male*	*Female*	*Children*
1.	Goldsmithy	Rs.1200.00	–	Rs. 300/-
2.	Carpentry	Rs.1500.00	–	–
3.	Blacksmithy	Rs. 800.00	Rs. 600.00	–
4.	Cobblery	Rs. 800.00	–	–
5.	Bamboo Basket Making	Rs. 700.00	–	–

Source: Field Survey.

Cobblers make desi chappals, water buckets and leather ornaments for cattle. Majority of these artisans are found in Dhone, Nandyal and Adoni Mandals. Depending upon the customer needs these cobblers earn a good part of their income, especially through the production of leather ornaments. They make ornaments chappals and shoes for auspicious occasions catering to the local taste. Bamboo basket makers make tubs and baskets of different sizes. They make these items colourfully. They also make tatties to cover the sides of huts and even for the purpose of roofs.

Some goldsmiths are experts in their trade and make silver and gold ornaments on prior orders. These artisans are mostly found in urban areas such as Adoni and Kurnool Revenue Mandals. They find these work in the areas where the purchasing power of the customers is very high.

The survey reveals that these artisans make traditional items to cater to the needs and tastes of local people. Little thought is bestowed on the improvement of their skill, and even on diversification of articles to make the items attractive or modern. Probably they are not interested in innovation and diversification in their trades, for there is no urban or modern influence on their trade. They seem to be satisfied with their traditional tools, methods of preparation and meagre incomes from their trades.

It is observed that most of the carpenters, blacksmiths and cobblers do not reveal their average income nor are they able to give definite opinion of their period of labour in a year. It is because of the fact that their customers are chiefly agriculturists who supply raw materials such as iron and steel and timber to them while placing orders for different articles. These artisans are satisfied with their labour charges on contract basis.

Now and then they incur minor expenses in the production of such items. The overall impression is such that these artisans have no zeal for specialisation in their trade. Probably the rural public do not expect modernised and attractive articles. The following Table 5.11 explains the quantity produced and the value of product.

Table 5.11: Articles Produced in Different Trades

Sl.No.	*Trade*	*Products*	*Quality Produced in a Year*	*Value (Rs)*
1.	Carpentry	a. Carts	24 Nos.	28,000.00
		b. Furniture	672 Nos.	46,000.00
		c. Agriculture Implements	367 Nos.	25,000.00
2.	Blacksmithy	a. Agriculture Implements	645 Nos.	14,900.00
		b. Buckets	120 Nos.	–
		c. Axes	530 Nos.	24,200.00
3.	Cobblery	a. Chappals	1450 Pairs	16,460.00
		b. Water Carriers	260 Nos.	4,550.00
		c. Shoes	254 Nos.	6,00.00
4.	Bamboo Basket Making	a. Basket gampa etc.	15,230 Nos.	16,106.00
5.	Goldsmithy	a. Ear rings	400 Pairs	8,00,000.00
		b. Nose rings	720 Nos.	3,60,000.00
		c. Bangles	1660 Nos.	33,60,000.00
		d. Pendants	142 Nos.	4,29,950.00
		e. Chains etc.	314 Nos.	3,42,620.00

Source: Field Survey.

Tools and Equipment

The tools and equipment used in different trades are of the value ranging from Rs. 400/- to Rs. 10,000/-. The tools and equipment commonly used in carpentry, and blacksmithy are wooden softener (The value of which ranges from Rs.100 to 150), handsaw (Rs. 80 to 100) chisel (Rs. 35 to 40), hammer (Rs. 40 to 50) and driller (Rs. 150 to 200), measuring scale (Rs. 25 to 40) blower (Rs. 35 to 45), Anvil (Rs. 100 to 120) grinder (Rs. 75 to 125) scissors and knife (Rs. 75 to 100) and files (Rs. 25 to 40).

These tools are of different sizes and temper. On an average the value of tools and equipment used by a carpenter is about Rs. 800/- and those of a blacksmith is Rs. 1200/-. The tools and equipment used by the carpenters of Atmakur and Velugodu Revenue Mandals are more in number and greater in value. The tools and equipment used by blacksmiths in Gudur, Nandikotkur and C' Belagal Revenue Mandals are of better quality than those used by others in other places. The carpenters cum blacksmiths use stronger and costlier tools and equipment. A master craftsman of this trade generally fabricates almost all the tools he needs.

A cobbler on an average possesses tools and equipment worth Rs. 400/-. The commonly used tools are a knife (Rs. 25 to 30), hammer (Rs. 30 to 40), stitching needle (Rs. 100), nail remover (Rs. 15 to 20), poker (Rs. 5 to 10), designer (Rs. 5 to 10), scissors (Rs. 25 to 40), sharpner (Rs. 50), metal base (Rs. 25), stool (Rs. 5) an earthen pot, a mhoti and hold all packet (Rs. 20 to 25).

Some cobblers use, sewing machine in their trade especially in Nandyal and Dhone Revenue Mandals. A machine costs about Rs. 5000. There are cobbler families who use only knife, hammer, pocker, stone and stitching needle, the total value of which does not exceed Rs. 250/-.

A goldsmith uses tools and equipment such as wheel blower costing Rs. 150 to 200, nose pilers Rs. 75, rough balance and weight Rs. 150 to 200, hammer of different sizes Rs. 40 to 70, scissors Rs. 40 to 70, cutting pliers Rs. 25 to 30 and measuring scale Rs. 20 to 25. The average cost of tools and equipment used in this trade is about Rs. 2500/-. The bamboo basket makers use a knife costing Rs. 25 to 35, wooden softner Rs. 25 to 45, measuring scale Rs. 10 to 15, file Rs. 10 to 20 and saw Rs. 25 to 40. The average value of these tools ranges from Rs. 150 to 200 per artisan.

It is observed that all these tools and equipment are traditional excepting sewing machine used by cobblers. An artisan of any trade uses modern or latest tools and equipment. On enquiry, it is found these artisans have neither inclination nor enthusiasm to improve their tools in light of the supply of machined instruments. They have no awareness of improved tools and equipments. Inspite of the present researcher's persistent encouragement they refuse to possess improved tools and equipment perhaps for the reason of paucity of funds. Table 5.12 furnishes value of tools and equipment used in different trades.

Marketing

The finished products made by these artisans have to get a sound market. Most of these items are sold in the local market. As these articles are produced to cater to the needs of agriculturists and consumers belonging to the rural areas, majority of these items are sold in the local market. Moreover many of them are produced on order or on contract basis. Only 18 per cent of these articles are sold outside the district. Even those articles are purchased mainly by wholesalers. Very negligible quantity of the product is sold out side the district direct to the consumers. Marketing of these products at distant places is an exception.

Agricultural implements, household furniture, buckets are manufactured or repaired for the local use. The articles made by blacksmiths and carpenters to a great extent are sold in the local market. However items produced by

Table 5.12: Value of Tools and Equipment used in Different Trade

Sl. No.	*Trade*	*Total*	*Tools and equipments*
1.	Carpentry	8,000.00	Wooden Softener, Saw Chisel, Hammer, Hand Driller, Scale, Blower, Dhakali Fixer.
2.	Blacksmithy	10,000.00	Hammer, Scissor, Wheel, Blower, Dhakali, Planer, Knives, Saw File, Metal Base.
3.	Cobblery	400.00	Knife, Hammer, Nail, remover, Stitching Needle, Metal Base, Stone, Designer, Magnet, Earthen Pot, Bucket, Sharper etc.
4.	Bamboo Basket Making	400.00	Knives, Wooden Softener, Scale File Handsaw.
5.	Goldsmithy	2500.00	Blowlamp, Hammers Set, Nose Pliers, Blower, Balance and Weights.

Source: Field Survey.

goldsmiths largely find market outside the rural area though within the district. Majority of these items find good market in the urban areas, either by direct sale to the consumer or through the wholesaler. In fact almost all these items are produced either on contract basis or on order. Generally contractors or the wholesalers supply raw materials to these artisans and procure the items manufactured by these artisans. Gold items are costly and so the artisans by themselves are not financially sound to produce and sell them direct to the consumers in the open market. Items belonging to agriculture and cobblery find a market only in the local areas. These items hardly find a market in the urban areas. Bamboo basket makers find rare chances for selling their product at distant places in the State. These items are mostly manufactured by the artisans with the raw materials purchased by themselves. The marketability of these items depend on an appreciation in rural and urban areas. These artisans transport their articles by carts and public convenience such as buses and mini lorries. The poor artisans wait in the road margin for a loaded lorry or a tempo or even a route bus for a long time with his articles and transport them to the urban areas. Transportation eats away a good percentage of the profit. At times the artisans sell their products at a loss to the wholesaler or the contractor. The following table reveals the details of marketability of these products in the local (rural area) markets and outside the district and state. Table 5.13 describes the marketing of products made by different artisans in the district in different destinations.

Financing of Rural Artisans

In any organised sector such as factory, corporation limited or unlimited concern, investment is not a very big problem. These business or production concerns can get financial assistance through banks or Central Government Department in the form of loan or subsidy respectively. But the trades under reference belong to unorganised individual entrepreneurs. The artisans have neither general education nor technical qualification. They are not trained in any recognised institution like ITI or Polytechnic. They are not certificate holder to get financial assistance from other agencies like banks and finance corporations nor are they rich enough to invest money in their trades. In fact these artisans need low cost technology and improved instruments and raw materials. They are not financially sound to invest money in this respect. They do not even get funds from private individuals or finance corporations at reasonable rates of interest. The Governmental agencies such as Department of Industries, Schedule Caste, Schedule Tribe Corporation and Backward Caste Corporation as well as State Finance Corporation come forward to give them financial aid. Lack of proper guidance, lack of free movement in the society and lack of education come in their way to procure financial assistance for investment both recurring and non recurring, and technical training. As there is no other way these illiterate artisans depend on moneylenders, who try to exploit them by exorbitant rates of interest, or purchasing their product at abnormally low price. Some of these artisans are deceived by

Table 5.13: Marketing by Destination of Products made by Artisans in Different Trades

Sl No.	Trade	Products	Local Market				Outside the village				Outside the district				Outside the state			
			Less than 25%	26% to 50%	51% to 75%	76% to 100%	Less than 25%	26% to 50%	51% to 75%	76% to 100%	Less than 25%	26% to 50%	51% to 75%	76% to 100%	Less than 25%	26% to 50%	51% to 75%	76% to 100%
1.	Carpentry	Carts, Furniture	20%	–	–	–	–	–	60%	–	20%	–	–	–	–	–	–	–
2.	Blacksmithy	Almirah, Plough Agriculture Implements	–	–	–	80%	20%	–	–	–	–	–	–	–	–	–	–	–
3.	Cobblery	Chappals, thondas etc.				80%	20%				–	–	–	–	–	–	–	–
4.	Bamboo Basket Making	Baskets, gampa, mats etc.			70%			30%		–	–	–	–	–	–	–	–	–
5.	Goldsmithy	Ear rings, nose rings, bangles, pendants, chains etc.		30%							–	–	70%	–	–	–	–	–
			30	30	70	160	40	30	60		20		70					
					52%				30%				18%					

Source: Field Survey.

middle men who promise to get loan from commercial banks and co-operative societies. The role of institution agencies in financing these artisans is very limited. As low as 11 per cent of artisans have borrowed funds from commercial banks: 18 per cent from Government agencies such as Adarana Scheme, Small Scale Industries department and so on, and 4 per cent artisans borrowed funds from money lenders. It is interesting to note that 67 per cent of these artisans have found their own methods of getting financial assistance. These artisans found bulk of the lot. They rise loans from friends and relatives hither and thither for a very short period, say, a couple of days or a week at an abnormally high rate of interest. Evidently they sell their products at very low prices so as to make it convenient for them to repay these temporary loans. These artisans get very limited profit and at times even losses. Their condition is deplorable. The following table 5.14 furnishes details.

Cost of Production

The average cost of production at work place is the highest in goldsmithy followed by carpentry, cobblery, blacksmithy and bamboo basket making in descending order. The cost of raw material in respect of goldsmithy is the highest, next comes carpentry, cobblery occupies the third place, while blacksmithy and bamboo basket making occupy fourth place and fifth place respectively. In this connection it is worthy to mention that carpentry incurs 7.9 per cent of expenditure for transportation, while bamboo basket makers expenditure on transportation is 4.14 per cent. In respect of goldsmithy expenditure on transportation is the least. It is only 0.42 per cent. Transportation expenditure on raw material belonging to Blacksmithy and Cobblery is nil. The cost of tools and machines in all these trades is very limited because all of them are of traditional type Table 5.15 is self explanatory.

Earning Capacity of the Artisans

The average number of persons involved at the work place in goldsmithy is the highest and that in cobblery

Table 5.14: Extent and Source of Institutional Assistance to Artisan in Different Trades

Sl. No.	Trade	No. of Artisans	Own Funds	Source of Assistance											
				Co. Op.		*Commercial Banks*		*Govt. I*		*Money Lenders*		*Friends Relatives*		*Other Specify*	
				Finance	*Raw Material*	*Finance*	*Raw Material*	*Finance*	*Raw Material*	*Finance*	*Raw Material*	*Finance*	*Raw Material*	*Finance*	*Raw Material*
1.	Carpentry	20	16 (80%)	–	–	2 (10%)	–	–	2 (10%)	–	–	–	–	–	–
2.	Blacksmithy	20	12 (60%)	–	–	–	–	4 (20%)	–	4 (20%)	–	–	–	–	–
3.	Cobblery	20	14 (70%)	–	–	–	–	6 (30%)	–	–	–	–	–	–	–
4.	Bamboo Basket Making	20	11 (55%)	–	–	–	9 (45%)	–	–	–	–	–	–	–	–
5.	Goldsmithy	20	14 (70%)	–	–	–	–	6 (30%)	–	–	–	–	–	–	–
		. 10	67	–	–	2	9	16	2	4	–	–	–	–	–

Source: Field Survey.

Table 5.15: Cost of Production

Sl. No.	*Type of artisan Activity*	*Raw Material*	*Wages*	*Fuel*	*Transport*	*Others Machanies*	*Tools*	*Total*
1.	Carpentry	1,64,327 (85%)	11,840 (6.12%)	400 (20%)	1,540 (79%)	–	16,231 (8.39%)	1,93,338
2.	Blacksmithy	61,144 (81%)	9,420 (12.84%)	1,255 (1.66%)	–	–	3,630.00 (4.81%)	75,449
3.	Cobblery	1,65,518 (94.66%)	5,525 (3.15%)	–	–	1,084 (0.61%)	2,720 (1.55%)	1,74,847
4.	Bamboo Basket Making	36,290 (75.21%)	6,000 (12.43%)	–	2000 (4.14)	–	3,960 (8.20%)	48,250
5.	Glodsmithy	26,25,918 (90.00%)	1,47,935 (5.07%)	64,119 (2.19%)	12,340 (0.42%)	38,856 (1.33%)	27,870 (0.95%)	29,17,038

Source: Field Survey.

blacksmithy and bamboo basket making is in the descending order. But the number of earners per family in bamboo basket making is the highest, followed by goldsmithy, blacksmithy, cobblery and carpentry. The average number of dependents on each earner in cobblery is the highest, followed by carpentry, goldsmithy, blacksmithy and bamboo basket making. As the number of persons involved in Cobblery at a work spot occupies the second place in gradation, it is interesting to note that the average number of dependents per earner is the highest. The average number of earners in a family in respect of carpentry is the lowest and the number of dependents per earner occupies second place in the gradation. Table 5.16 explains the earning capacity of the artisans.

Table 5.16: Family Size and the Number of Earners

Sl. No.	*Trade*	*Average No. of persons per artisan family*	*Average No. of earners per artisan family*	*Number of dependents per earner*
1.	Carpentry	5	1	4
2.	Blacksmithy	6	4	2
3.	Cobblery	7	2	5
4.	Bamboo Basket Making	6	2	4
5.	Glodsmithy	8	3	5

Source: Field Survey.

Scope for Technological Transformation of Rural Artisan Trades

All these artisans use crude type of instruments in their trades. Inspite of the fact that they know that modern technological and skilled equipment is available now-a-days, they do not go in for these improved implements. Awareness alone can not translate their wishes into a reality. Though some of these artisans are not ready to receive these improved implements, most of them find it very difficult to procure them, because of their poor financial condition. However, blacksmiths are not aware of any such possibility. Bamboo basket makers, cobblers and goldsmiths to a very great extent express their willingness to switch over to the new technology. Very few artisans in respect of carpentry and goldsmithy have procured some of the new implements for their use.

These artisans are not trained to use the modern technical equipment in their trades. There is a dire necessity for the improvement of their skills in their respective trades. The improved hand tools and some of the mechanically operated tools have come into the market. These trends are not in effective use among the artisans. In spite of training given under TRYSEM of the DRDA and Adarana Pathakam, these artisans are not properly enlightened. Many of these artisans do not undergo training regularly and even if they undergo, they do not pay due attention to the use of modern equipment. As a result the finished product of these artisans is unable to compete in the market with other product produced with the help of modern equipment by the ITI trained and other skilled artisans. The Government agencies like TRYSEM and Adarana give training to these artisans and at the end of training period, modern implements are supplied to the artisans at subsidised rates. It is deplorable to note that these artisans even after the training resort to old methods. The financial conditions are not thereby improved Table 5.17 lists out improved tool kits for the artisans.

Problems in Popularising Improved Tool Kits

Detailed survey in Kurnool District reveals that most of the artisans are not ready to embrace new technique and improved tool kits for use in their trades. 10 per cent of the artisans refuse to respond to questions posed by the surveyor, Artisans in carpentry, blacksmithy, cobblery, bamboo basket making, goldsmithy have received training and used technical implements to a tune of 27 per cent. On account of lack of

Table 5.17: Improved Took Kits For The Artisans

Sl.No.	*Name of the Trade*	*Name of the improved Tool Kits*
1.	Carpentrey	1. Rallys wold hard drilling machine (power operation). 2. Shash Bar gram –6 Ft 2 Nos. 3. Half round wood rough files 10 inches. 4. Round files-rough, smooth 1 No. 5. G. Clamps 8 inches, 6 inches 4 Nos. 6. Chisels 1/4 to 2" 1 set 7. Augers 1/8 to 3/4 1 set. 8. Planes 2 Nos. 9. Bench vice 1 No. 10. Trysquare 11. Foot rules-wooden 2 Nos. 12. Cutting pliers steel 2 Nos. 13. Pincers - 2 Nos. 14. Hand saw 2 Ft. 1 No. 15. Tenson saw 1.4 ft 1 No. 16. Fret Saw 1 No.
2.	Blacksmithy	1. Blower (18 with 1/2 HP motor) 2. Sewage block 1 Cwt. 3. Sludge Hammer 1 No. 4. Ankil with stteep top 1 Cwt. 5. Double handed hand hammer 2 Nos. 6. Tonges 1 No. 7. Let vice 1 No. 8. Hot chiesels 1 Set. 9. Spanner set 1 No.
3.	Cobblery	Cutting knives, rampiece, iron-tray-leg, hammer, cuttingplier, pincer, oil stone, eye letting set, bruches.
4.	Bamboo Basket Making	Tools, designed by all India Handicrafts Board.
5.	Goldsmithy	Blow lamp, small anvil, hammers set nosepliers, blower, foreceps, moulds, balances and weights.

Source: Field Survey.

finance, 32 per cent of these artisans do not buy the new equipment though they are in favour of such improved equipment in their trades. Only 23 per cent of the artisans were trained in the use of modern equipment in their trades. Unfortunately we find very insignificant percentage of artisans who have procured licence from Department of Industries. This is a really unimaginably low percentage. If better facilities are made available for training and if improved tool kits are supplied and if the Department of Industries takes special drive for grant of licences to these artisans there is a great possibility of getting these problems and short comings obviated. Table 5.18 gives the details.

Unit Cost of Production and Selling Price of Different Items made in Trades

A cart is sold at a value of Rs. 8000/- to Rs. 8500/-, depending upon its type and size. A carpenter or a carpenter cum-blacksmith incurs an expenditure of Rs. 5500/- to 6000/- on each cart. He charges marginal profit of Rs. 2000/- to Rs. 2500/- on each cart and sells the finished goods at Rs. 8000/- to Rs. 8500/- each. There will be an average marginal profit of Rs. 1500/- on each cart. In respect of household furniture the cost of a Chair, table or almirah ranges from Rs. 250/- to Rs. 300/-, from Rs. 400/- to Rs. 450/- and from Rs. 150/- to Rs. 175/- respectively. The carpenter sells these items with the marginal profit of Rs. 50/- on each item on an average. However in respect of horse shoes and Ox shoes there will be Rs. 100/- profit, but in case of buckets and axes he gets a profit from 25 to 30 per cent.

In cobblery, production of chappals is predominant. Water carriers and motas (large buckets for drawing up water from a well) leather ornaments for cattle (Thondas) are also manufactured. The cost of a pair of chappals ranges from Rs. 50/- and Rs. 75/- depending upon the size and type. The selling price of the pair is between Rs. 75/- and Rs. 100/-, depending upon the customers and the type and quality of chappals. A cobbler gets a marginal profit ranging from

Table 5.18: Problems of Implementing Improved Tool Kits

Sl. No.	*Type of Artisan Activity*	*Lack of Money*	*No. Training*	*No Licence*	*Not in favour of new tool kits*	*No response*	*Total*
1.	Carpentry	3 (15%)	4 (20%)	2 (10%)	8 (40%)	3 (15%)	20
2.	Blacksmithy	5 (25%)	6 (30%)	1 (5%)	6 (30%)	2 (10%)	20
3.	Cobblery	8 (40%)	4 (20%)	2 (10%)	5 (25%)	1 (5%)	20
4.	Bamboo Basket Making	9 (45%)	4 (20%)	1 (5%)	4 (20%)	2 (10%)	20
5.	Goldsmithy	7 (35%)	5 (25%)	2 (10%)	4 (20%)	2 (10%)	20
		32	23	8	27	10	100

Source: Field Survey.

Rs. 50/- to Rs. 100/- on each pair. Generally leather ornaments for cattle are made on order. A set of these ornaments costs ranging from Rs. 150/- to Rs. 200/- and the selling price ranges from Rs. 200/- to Rs. 250/-. Evidently a cobbler gets a marginal profit ranging from 20 to 30 per cent. Some cobblers buy untanned hides and skins of animals and tan them in their own crude manner and utilise them for manufacturing purposes in their trade—reins and saddles and other decorative materials for animals. Some of these crudely tanned skin articles are sold in the market near by.

Bamboo basket makers spend Rs. 15/- to 20/- on each basket, gampa or similar article depending upon its size and thickness. He sells such items at Rs. 20/- to Rs. 25/-. The marginal profit is about 25 per cent. These artisans are found in Atmakur and Velugodu Revenue Mandals.

Goldsmithy is a costly trade involving honesty, skill and capacity to invest huge amounts. Cost of gold generally fluctuates from time to time. Therefore no goldsmith takes the risk of manufacturing items by investing his own money. Generally he undertakes the manufacturing of any item on order. He takes Gold from the person who needs an item of gold. In such cases of individual customers, 11.666 grams of Gold is blended with only 1.1 grams of copper and an ornament is made of the alloy. For public sale 11.666 grams of gold is blended with 1.46 grams of copper and an ornament is made. Again if the former item is purchased by the goldsmith from the customer, he values the items as per the latter norm, thereby the goldsmith gets a profit of 0.36 grams of gold per 11.666 grams of gold. In this respect the goldsmith charges his labour and also gets 1 gram of gold per 11.666 grams of gold under wastage. Thus goldsmithy is a profitable trade and a dignified job in the rural and urban areas. Generally a skillful goldsmith gets a marginal profit of 14 to 16 per cent. As the turnover is heavy the profits also are considerably large. The cost and selling price of any ornament is in large proportion. However, if the customer delays to take delivery of ornaments from the goldsmith, the latter is likely to incur a loss of interest on the investment. Therefore, generally the customer is requested to invest the amount on gold and give the design and model to the goldsmith. The following table 5.19 explains the cost of production and the selling price of different items made by the artisans.

Table 5.19: Unit Cost of Production and Selling Price of Different Items made in Trades.

Sl.No.	*Trade*		*Products*	*Cost per unit Rs.*	*Selling Price Rs*
1.	Carpentry	*(i)*	Cart	5500 to 6000	8000 to 8500
		(ii)	Chair	250 to 300	350 to 400
		(iii)	Tables	400 to 450	450 to 500
2.	Blacksmithy	*(i)*	Almirah	150 to 175	200 to 225
		(ii)	Plough	50 to 60	75 to 100
3.	Cobblery	*(i)*	Chappals	100 to 120	120 to 150
		(ii)	Thondas	150 to 200	200 to 250
		(iii)	Motes	300 to 350	450 to 500
4.	Bamboo Basket Making	*(i)*	Baskets	10 to 15	15 to 20
		(ii)	Gampa	20 to 25	25 to 30
5.	Goldsmithy	*(i)*	Ear rings	2000 to 2200	2500 to 2700
		(ii)	Nose rings	1000 to 1200	1200 to 1250
		(iii)	Bangles (each)	5000 to 5100	5500 to 5600
		(iv)	Chains etc.	5000 to 5100	5500 to 5600

Source: Field Survey.

In respect of household furniture such as chairs, tables and almirahs, the cost ranges from Rs. 250/-, Rs. 300/-, Rs. 400/-, Rs. 450/-, Rs. 150/-, Rs. 175/-. The ultimate price comes to Rs. 350/-, Rs. 400/-, Rs. 450/-, Rs. 500/-, Rs. 200/-, Rs. 225/- respectively. On an average the artisans margin is around to Rs. 100/- per chair, Rs. 100/- per table and Rs. 25/- per each pair of horse shoes and oxen shoes over 100 per cent, buckets and axes between 25 and 30 per cent.

In Cobblery, production of chappals takes a predominant place. Water carriers are also very costly. Cost per pair of chappals varies from Rs. 50/- to Rs. 75/- for different sizes. The consumer price also varies between Rs. 75/- and Rs. 100/- Margin of profit thus ranges from Rs. 50/- to Rs. 100/- depending upon quality and type of customers. The leather ornaments for cattle (Thondas) are made at a cost ranging from Rs. 150/- to Rs. 200/- and sold to the customers at Rs. 200/- to Rs. 250/-. The Cobblers ordinarily seem to have a margin of 20 to 30 per cent. They mostly buy the crudely tanned tides and skins some of them process themselves in a very poor way and either use it themselves or sell to fellow cobblers in the craft. Other material such as nails, plastic and rexin sheets etc. are purchased from near by urban areas.

The Bamboo Basket makers make baskets, gampa and other articles. A Basket costs anywhere between Rs. 15/- and Rs. 20/- each depending on size. A gampa Rs. 20/- and Rs. 25/-. The artisans in Atmakur and Velugodu Revenue Mandals produce more than others.

In respect of goldsmith 12 Grams of gold valued Rs. 5000/- to Rs. 5500/-. It is reported that ornaments are prepared on the basis of the Interest of the consumers. Several types of ornaments are prepared like ear rings, nose ring, bangles, chains, etc. The artisans in this trade work occasionally.

The Problems

In the preceding paragraphs, several aspects such as production and items produced, employment, marketing, tools and equipment etc. of the selected trades in the district as also the social and economic status of the artisans and their families are dealt with. Extent of institutional assistance at present is also discussed. The one impression that the analysis makes is that all is not well either with the artisans or the trades. The trades are almost wholly traditional, turning out traditional articles, with traditional tools and equipment, limited marketing and inadequate income. In this background one can as well fancy the economic conditions of hundreds of artisans and their families with these trades as the main or only source of livelihood. There is a vast degree of underemployment. There are limited opportunities for alternative and subsidiary occupations. Some artisans seem to persist in their respective trades with the least initiative either for improvement in skill or for better techniques of production and marketing. A majority of them have shown the grit to pull along. Under the circumstances, it is the government and co-operative institutions that can do a lot for the helpless hundreds. Should the analysis of institutional assistance be any indicator, it follows that there is a vast percentage of artisan population that remains untouched by institutional assistance rendered so far. Problems continue to haunt them. Table 5.20 briefly summarizes their problems.

As per the given data, nearly 80 per cent of the artisans under study, experience financial shortage in varying degrees. Almost all the artisans in the different trades have expressed their financial needs as most pressing either to buy tools and equipment of improved variety or raw materials or finance for marketing. It is also true that most of them require consumption finance as is clear from income analysis. Perhaps, data on assets and liabilities would have thrown more light.

The next important problem faced by the artisans is demand or market for their articles. 17 per cent of artisans representing all trades have this problem. To recapitulate, nearly 17 per cent of the artisans, excepting majority of carpenters and cobblers who produce articles in anticipation of demand and a slightly lesser percentage work on contract. Other partly undertake contract job and partly anticipate market for the goods already produced.

Another serious problem faced by many artisans, is procurement of raw materials. Barring majority of carpenters, bamboo basket making, raw material is in short supply and is not easily available at a reasonable price to

Table 5.20: Artisans and their Problems

Sl. No.	*Trade*	*No. of Artisans*	*Problems*								
			Financial	*Raw Material*	*Market*	*Labour*	*Demand*	*Transport*	*Govt. Policies*	*Power*	*Other*
1.	Carpentry	20	8 (46%)	4 (20%)	6 (30%)	4 (20%)	4 (20%)	2 (10%)	–	–	–
2.	Blacksmithy	20	9 (45%)	5 (25%)	8 (40%)	2 (15%)	–	–	–	–	3 (15%)
3.	Cobblery	20	12 (60%)	4 (20%)	3 (15%)	–	5 (25%)	–	–	–	2 (10%)
4.	Bamboo Basket Making	20	9 (45%)	9 (45%)	4 (20%)	–	4 (20%)	2 (10)	–	–	–
5.	Goldsmithy	20	8 (40%)	–	4 (20%)	2 (10%)	4 (20%)	–	6 (30%)	2 (10%)	–
		100	46	22	25	8	17	4	6	2	5

Source: Field Survey.

many others. Customers supply the necessary iron and steel and timber while placing orders with the carpenters and blacksmiths. The cobblers hunt after hides and skin themselves, attempt crude tanning and utilise the same in their work. Even so they experience shortage of the material. Further, for goldsmiths, the basic material is not locally available. Thus 22 per cent of artisans encounter raw material difficulty either as its shortage or as its availability at a high price. These problems are present in varying degrees for all the trades.

In addition, some artisans engaged in carpentry, bamboo basket making, goldsmith have reported other problems. The carpenter, and bamboo basket maker have transport problem. Some of them also need improved tools and equipment and marketing assistance. The carpenters and blacksmiths need both marketing assistance and improved tools and equipment. The cobblers need training facilities and extension service. They also urge for the supply of better tools. The goldsmith seems to be inconvenienced by Government policies and power shortage.

Thus problems are multifarious and need timely and adequate attention. The situation demands a bold and practical prescription, preferably on institutional basis to relieve the several hundreds of artisans from the apathy and eternal poverty to which they have been subjected. See Table 5.20.

6

Summary and Suggestions

This Chapter presents a summary of the findings, besides some pragmatic suggestions with reference to the artisans in Kurnool District.

This study makes an attempt to evaluate the socio economic conditions of artisans and the impact of the financial assistance, provided by the Government to artisans in the creation of remunerative employment opportunities and generation of additional income to artisans in Kurnool district. No such study has been attempted so far in Kurnool district in the past. The glory of the artisans in the past and their present plight are held in focus in the study. The efforts of the Government to rehabilitate the poor artisans are highlighted.

Economic planning is an Instrument in the hands of the Economists to achieve economic aspirations of people. Planning for the development of artisans also helps in ushering an era of prosperity for them. Many schemes have been designed during Five Year Plans for providing adequate finance to poor artisans.

Finance is very essential for the development of a country in general, industry, commerce and trade in particular. Timely and adequate financial assistance accelerates the growth of major, medium, and small scale and cottage industries in case of artisans and small entrepreneurs it is more so. Adequate finance provided to artisans helps to increase employment opportunities, productivity and income. This is possible through institutional finance such as Government, Nationalised Banks, and other Commercial Banks.

The area of study covers 5 trades situated in 10 Revenue Mandals of Kurnool district. The sample covers 100 artisans belonging to five different trades and records their conditions and responses.

The statistical data for the study is collected with the help of a systematically designed schedule. The data collected is analysed and presented in suitable tables to interpret the impact of artisans on the creation of gainful employment.

The socio economic status of the selected artisan groups differs to a great extent from one another. In the social hierarchy, the economically backward caste comes first followed by the Backward Castes, Scheduled Castes and Scheduled Tribes in the descending order. From the economic point of view, the economic status of all the five artisan groups is more or less the same.

The educational status of the respondents is very discouraging. It is very low, in general among all the respondents under study. From among the artisans of different groups 40 per cent are illiterates. 7 per cent have attended primary school, 8 per cent have attended secondary school and 45 per cent have formal education. The educational backwardness is further contributing to their socio economic deprivation.

The respondents are following various occupations. They comprise carpenters; blacksmiths; cobblers; bamboo basket makers and goldsmiths.

Regarding land holdings, all the respondents belonging to economically backward caste possess landed property. The land holdings by the respondents are very low, small and uneconomic. Therefore there is a need to create alternative employment opportunities outside agriculture.

In the study area the employment opportunities created through artisan are considerable. The analysis of these data shows the financial assistance provided by the Government. Regarding the loans issued to artisans, more than seventy per cent of the artisans are of the opinion that the financial assistance provided is not adequate to meet their genuine demands.

Regarding the effect of financial assistance of Government on employment and output, positive trends are observed in the study. The additional employment opportunities created by the assistance of the Government are helping to increase labour productivity and production among the artisans.

Problems of Rural Artisans

Most of the problems that are being faced by the rural artisans emerge from the conditions in which the artisans are placed. The rural artisans – poor, scattered, unorganised and illiterate, - have poor productive asset base, — use outmoded equipment, are exploited by usurious middlemen, contractors and master artisans, they do not have the benefit of an organised market and depend on private marketing system.

There has been an increase in the number of schemes and institutions to help the artisans, but there are no adequate arrangements for co-ordination and monitoring of these schemes. Further, most of the artisans and small entrepreneurs fail to get a package of services, especially scarce raw materials. Economic prosperity of farmers has changed their consumption requirements. Manufactured commodities of industry are cheap and refined as compared with goods produced by local artisans. Hence the artisans have no option but gradually shift to other occupations.

The rural artisans suffer from lack of financial resources at their disposal. They work more in their own houses, which are very small. Most of the artisans are compelled to shift from their traditional occupations to other professions for their livelihood. It is essential to give due emphasis to skill formation in rural artisans. Even those who are able to upgrade their skills are also facing some problems.

(i) Non-availability of financial resources to purchase new tools.

(ii) Lack of awareness of entrepreneurial and management problems involved in setting up of an industry.

(iii) Lack of marketing ability and

(iv) Inability to derive much benefit from the facilities created for the development of artisans under various programmes.

The artisans are facing special problems in procuring raw materials. There is substantial competition from the organised sector, which has, to a great extent, affected the regular and assured supply of raw materials. Middlemen, who supply raw materials, usually tend to exploit artisans in a number of ways.

Marketing a product subsequently becomes a major problem for the rural artisans. The artisans lack staying power and are also ignorant of the true market potential and are unable to tap the same to establish a market for their product. Government assistance in the form of sales through State-owned corporations and emporia is leading artisans to a better life, which was earlier not available to artisans in the rural sector.

Most artisan enterprises lack the requisite managerial and technical expertise. Most units suffer from poor planning and execution of programmes.

Other problems include outdated designs and models and the lack of market intelligence.

One of the major problems inherent in the village and small industries, particularly the traditional industries, has been the lack of adequate finance. The lack of an effective system of financing these units through institutional sources has been the major obstacle in the development and growth of this sector. Infrastructural constraints include a host of problems like banking, transportation, warehousing and marketing facilities, obsolete technology inadequate and irregular supply of raw materials and other critical inputs, lack of managerial and technical expertise etc.

One of the daunting problems facing small units in rural areas is that of obsolete technology. Obsolete technology has a very important bearing on the productivity and cost aspects. The Technology adopted also has an impact on the quality of the output Deterioration in the quality of output due to the use of outdated and manual methods of production is, therefore, a major impediment in expanding the market for products of the small units.

Transportation difficulties are experienced by certain category of artisans in transporting their finished goods as well as raw materials. Artisans like, carpenters, bamboo basket makers, cobblers experience this problem. It is reported that carpenters while bringing raw materials by vehicle face serious difficulties. They also experience similar difficulties while transporting their finished goods.

Almost all the artisan vocations in the selected areas have traditional and low skilled jobs. The only asset to the artisans is his skill. The work of the artisans and production depends on the level of his skill, experience and knowledge he possesses of the profession. Out of the 100 artisan samples studied 92 practice traditional and inherited skills. They have not received any formal training though the facilities are available to them. Only 8 of the artisans practise skills acquired through formal training in established institutions. Almost all the artisans under consideration use traditional and old tools in their productive activities. This is mainly responsible for their low productivity and output. Modern tools are not used by them for lack of training and knowledge about them. Meager financial resources, inadequate professional skill, low level of education, lack of interest to improve their method of operation have all contributed to this state of affairs. Hence the artisans are caught in the whirlpool of low productivity and low incomes.

The incomes of rural artisan households are generally low. The borrowed amounts are not put to productive uses by them. According to the study, majority of the sample artisans have used the borrowed amount for non-productive purposes particularly towards individual consumption purposes.

The rural artisans depend both on institutional and non-institutional sources for their working capital requirements. There is no exact estimate of the working capital lent to rural artisans. This estimate needs to be done to ascertain the economic feasibility of the artisan's projects in the plan.

Besides, institutional credit provided is inadequate. It is also not provided at the right time. An important factor contributing to the non-viability of artisan enterprises is lack of adequate working capital. The study reveals that the requirement of working capital of a rural artisan ranges between Rs.500 in bamboo basket making industry and Rs.8000 in carpentry depending on seasons for raw materials and marketing. In some cases like blacksmith and cobblers the working capital requirement is estimated to be Rs.7000 and Rs.8000 respectively.

Inadequate credit is the cause for low financial returns. When the artisans get money after the seasons, they spend it for non-productive purposes and are labelled as defaulters. Lack of entrepreneurial skill which continues to be a major problem should be tackled through proper monitoring by agencies, guidance and training facilities.

Even where there is provision for sanctioning a second loan, it is not of much help to the artisans. Very often the second loan is adjusted by the banker towards the repayment of the first loan as he is under pressure to show progress in respect of loan recovery.

As the rural artisans face a number of problems, there must be appropriate institutional agencies to help them. In most States, though a few agencies have been created, they lack co-ordination and in many cases, the artisans have failed to utilise the facilities provided by such organisations.

Suggestions to Improve Artisan's Conditions

Most artisans face the problem of inadequate accommodation. The artisans must be provided with house sites through housing co-operative societies or Government housing schemes. Training institutions should be involved in training the artisans with the main purpose of upgrading skills to enable them to handle jobs requiring better skills. Financial institutions should take increasing interest in helping the artisans and well established links between the artisans and co-operative, rural banks and commercial banks should be well established through the agency formed to help the artisans. Introduction and popularisation of new designs to cater to the increasing domestic demand and export demand will have to be attempted in various trades.

The District Industries Centres have to help the artisans in a big way. Some immediate measures to help the artisans are:

Artisans from at least 10 villages should form professional associations under the leadership of responsible persons having some background in social work, preferably from amongst themselves. The leadership should bring them together, for a unified effort to claim and avail themselves of the benefits from various development programmes sponsored by the Government.

Facilities of technical education and training should be made available to the artisan groups by considering them weaker sections of the society;

Schemes for providing subsidies to artisans to enable them to upgrade production to the level of small-scale industries should be worked out and implemented. Under these schemes, tools machinery, raw materials etc., should be provided to them with some guidance in management etc.

Efforts to impart theoretical/academic knowledge to the artisans through mass media may be made so that they are able to push up their productive potentialities.

Banks have rightly thought of financing village craft industries and services as they have a large employment potential. Assistance from banks to rural artisans should be on the following lines.

Commercial banks should equip themselves with technical and trained manpower to deal with rural artisans. Certain percentage of total bank credit should be earmarked specifically for financing rural artisans as a part of integrated development programmes.

Extensive surveys should be conducted to identify artisans block-wise and trade-wise and also the number of artisans assisted by commercial banks under different programmes;

Research studies evaluating the impact of bank credit on asset-base, income and employment generation are of great importance;

Artisans' co-operatives should also be financed in addition to financing individual artisans;

Banks need not favour artisans having assets. In fact, the purpose of the financial assistance by banks aims at strengthening the productive asset-base of the rural poor;

Financial assistance should be given for establishing market-cum-service centres which act as multi-functional centres and serve as centres of guidance to the rural artisans; and

Area-specific schemes should be drawn up and financed so that such crafts could be preserved and their employment possibilities be fully exploited.

The Composite Term Loan Scheme, which was framed in 1979, took into account the total financial needs of the rural artisans in village and cottage industries. Under this scheme, units set-up in villages and towns with a population not exceeding 50,000 and which used local resources are eligible for loans not exceeding Rs. 25,000 at concessional rates of interest. To meet the consumption needs of the artisans, a consumption loan not exceeding Rs. 500 was also granted under the scheme. The loans could be repaid over a long period of seven-to-ten years in small instalments, depending on the surplus generated, after an initial moratorium of 12 to 18 months.

The rural artisans whose annual family income does not exceed Rs. 6,400 (Rs. 7,200 in urban and metropolitan areas) are extended financial assistance up to Rs. 6,500 under the Differential Interest Rate (DIR) Scheme at four per cent interest for working capital as well as for acquiring appropriate equipment.

In 1984, NABARD announced a new scheme providing term loans of Rs.10,000 to rural artisans at 10 per cent interest. The repayment period varied from three-to ten years depending on the customer's repayment capacity. NABARD's refinance scheme covers settlements with population upto 10,000. Refinance is available to primary lending institutions for infrastructural support proposed for the rural artisan's sector in centres with population upto 50,000.

NABARD, in the 1996-97 fiscal, has been sanctioned Rs. 500 crore as advance additional share capital, Rs. 100 crore by the government and Rs. 400 crore by the Reserve Bank of India (RBI). The above mentioned share capital will be augmented by similar amount of Rs. 500 crore as announced by the Union Finance Minister P. Chidambaram in the 1997-98 Union Budget. The amount would be for the 1997-98 fiscal.

For increasing the viability of both enterprise and credit, provision should be made for entrepreneurial training to borrowers and some special training to the bank employees for monitoring the rural industries including rural orientation programmes.

The whole training curriculum should be based on the philosophy that an attitudinal change is indispensable for the rural artisans to make the best use of the facilities provided to them.

Artisans' training in the Khadi and Village Industries (KVI) sector is arranged mostly through institutions engaged in the development of the industry. It is in-plant training with emphasis on learning by doing rather than by instruction.

The rural artisans to a great extent depend on out-dated technology, resulting in failure to avail themselves of the economic liberalisation. They required technology to tap the existing local resources and equal to sustain the environmental conditions. There is a need to develop an effective linkage of modern science and technology with the rural community, focusing mainly on rural industries and village artisans.

The process of adaptation of modern technology to suit the conditions prevalent in rural India has begun on a modest scale which emphasizes the needs to evolve a strategy for blending the traditional and modern technologies in the context of local requirements.

Artisans and craftsmen should be given the opportunities to receive new technologies first and then transfer them to user groups in villages through systematised liaison with R&D agencies. The artisan, after acquiring training, tools, and raw materials should be encouraged to use the acquired skills to benefit other user groups.

Technology transfer becomes easier because the artisan is born and brought up in the village and his language and culture are those of the user groups. Also, if there is anything wrong with the technology, the user can approach the artisan immediately in the village itself and ask him to amend or modify the technology at short notice.

The Rural Artisans Programmes (RAP) was launched in 1971-72 as part of the Small Farmers' Development Agency (SFDA) and Marginal Farmers and Agricultural Labourers Development Agency (MFALDA). RAP was started in 87 selected areas all over India and it was handled by the Development Commissioner, Small-Scale Industries, Later on the programme was taken over by the District Industries Centres (DICs).

The Rural Artisan Programmes aim at providing training in varying skills so as to induce in artisans the urge to acquire new skills and open up opportunities to take up small enterprises, primarily to meet local needs, with improved tools. Rural Artisan Programmes give priority to village trades like poultry, masonry, carpentry, blacksmithy, repair and maintenance of agricultural implements, machinery, tractors, pumpsets, diesel engines and electric fittings. Rural Artisan Programmes provide subsidy to artisans to help them stabilise in their chosen professions. The subsidies may be of different kinds like tool kits, plant and equipment, managerial subsidy and subsidy for worksheds.

The Rural Artisan Complexes (RACs) emerged were set up on the outskirts of villages during 1981 with a view to providing better living and working conditions to those artisans who lacked accommodation in their village each Rural Artisan Complexes accommodate at least 20 artisans. The unifunctional complex accommodates artisans from the same trade while multi-functional ones accommodate artisans from diverse trades. Priority should be given to integrate Rural Artisan Complexes programme with rural housing schemes.

The artisan development programmes receive help not only from the DICs, but also other agencies like District Rural Development Agency (DRDA) the Khadi and Village Industries Commission/Boards and Handicrafts/Handloom Boards. But, proper co-ordination is lacking in formulating and implementing programmes for the benefit of rural artisans.

The DICs conduct detailed surveys to identify artisans and also the type of training needed by them. The training programme is arranged on the spot for those who require training for a short period, say a fortnight. For others, requiring training for three months to one year, the same is arranged on priority basis in suitable institutions. Occasionally training is imparted in industrial units also.

There is a need for improving the financial viability and sustainability of various schemes. Measures should be initiated to improve extension services to promote artisan based activities to enable them to tap the domestic as well as foreign market for their products. There is also a need for developing service-type rural artisan trades. The artisans can survive in a competitive world only when they possess the capacity to diversify and modernise their skills in time with the present needs. The needs of the modern rural consumer are changing fast. Of course, area specific schemes should be drawn up and effectively implemented. The artisans may form co-operatives to take advantage on several fronts, particularly marketing.

What the rural artisans urgently require is a package of services which include training, new designs, raw materials, credit, marketing and general guidance.

Bibliography

Books

Abdul Aziz. The Rural Poor: Problems and Prospects, Ashish Publishing House, New Delhi,1983.

Akram, S., Development of Small Scale Industries in Bihar, Delhi, Capital Publishing House, 1984.

Alexander, R.J., "A Primer to Economic Development" the Macmillan and Co., London, 1962.

Anderson Dennis, Finian Cuig Small Scale Industry and Agriculture in Development Countries, World Bank Staff Working Paper, 519, Washington, 1982.

Balasa, "The Process of Industrial Development and Alternative Development Strategy" World Bank Staff Working Papers, 1980.

Bama, D.S., "New Strategy for Industrial Development of Flood and Drought Prone Area" Hauz Khas Enclave, New Delhi, 1970.

Baner, P.F. and Yemey, B.S., "The Economics of under developed countries, Cambridge University Press, London, 1965.

Bhattacharya, S.N., "Development of Industrial Backward Area" (The Indian Style) Metropolitan, Pragati Press, through V.R.N. Composing Agency, Delhi, 1981.

Chowdary Muktar Singh: Cottage and Small Scale Industries, Kitabistam Publishers, Allahabad 1987.

Coldar, B.N., Productivity Growth in Indian Industry, New Delhi, Allied Publishers Pvt. Ltd., 1986.

Cykor, G., Strategies for Industrialisation in Developing Countries, C. Hurst and Co., London 1974.

Desai Vasnth, "Problems and Prospects of Small Scale Industries, "Himalaya Publishing House, Bombay, 1983.

Dhar P.N., and Lyndall, H.T., "The Role of Small Enterprises in Indian Economic Development", Asia Publishing House, Bombay, 1961.

Dobb, "Economic Growth and Under Developed Countries", London, 1953.

Everett E., Mage, "Hand Book for Industry Studies" Asia Publishing House, New Delhi, 1959.

Farooque, Q.H. Small Scale and Cottage Industries as a means of providing opportunities for labour in India, Agra University, 1958.

Godbole, M.D., Industrial Dispersal Policies, Bombay, Himalaya Publishing House, 1979.

George Rosen, 'Industrial Change in India", Asia Publishing House, New Delhi, 1959.

Government of India, A Hand Book: Extension Services for Rural Industrial Development, New Delhi, Development Commissioner, Small Scale Industries, 1980.

Government of India, Small Scale Industries in Indian Policies, Programmes and Institutional Support, New Delhi, Development Commissioner, Small Scale Industries, 1982.

Gunnar Myrdal, "Economic Theory and Under Developed Regions" Vora and Co., Publishing (P) Ltd., Bombay, 1958.

Halfman, W.G., The Growth of Industrial Economics, Oxford University Press, 1958.

ICSSR, "A Survey of Research in Economics, Vol., V. Allied Publishers, New Delhi, 1975.

Industrial Development Bank of India, Industrial Development of Backward Areas, Bombay, IDBI, 1981.

Iyer Ganapati, E.V., Indian Industrial Development Its problems, Ganapati Trans west, Bangalore, Association Pvt. Ltd., 1986.

Isard, W., "Methods of Regional Analysis" An Introduction to Regional Science, Wiley New York, 1960.

Iyer Krishna, T.N., Guideline for Fianncing of Small Scale Industries. A Hand Book for Bankers, Bombay, Sevak Prakasam, 1980.

Jain, P.C., "Industrial Problems of India" Kitabistan, Allahabad, 1942.

James. C. Van Home: Financial Management in Policy Printice Hall of India, New Delhi, 1974.

Joshi, Navain, C. Cottage and Small Scale Industry in India, Suneja Book Centre, New Delhi, 1956.

Kaur Kula Winder, Structure of Industries in India, New Delhi, Deep and Deep Publications, 1981.

Killy, P., "Small Scale Industry in Kenya", IBRD (Mimeo) Development Economics Department, 1981.

Kirpatrick, C.H., and N. Lee and F.I. Nixon, Industrial Structure and Police in Less Development Countries, New Delhi, Heritage Publishers, 185.

Kuznets, Simon, Modern Economic Growth, New Delhi, Oxfords I.B.H. Publishing Co., 1965.

Lakshmana Rao, V., "Economic Development of Andhra Pradesh", R.R. Publishing Corporation, Delhi, 1985.

Lakshmi Narasaiah M, "Growth and Performance of Small Scale Industries", New Delhi, Discovery Publishing House, 1999.

Lakshmi Narasaiah. M, "Small Scale Industry", New Delhi, Discovery Publishing House, 1999.

Lakshmi Narasaiah M., "Industrial Development", New Delhi, Discovery Publishing House, New Delhi, 1999.

Lakshmi Narasaiah. M, "Industrialisation in backward areas, New Delhi, Discovery Publishing, House, New Delhi, 2001.

Lakshmi Narasaiah. M, "Small Scale Entrepreneurship", New Delhi, Discovery Publishing House, 2001.

Lakshmi Narasaiah. M, "Small Scale Entrepreneurship", New Delhi, Discovery Publishing House, 2002.

Little lan, M.D. Et Al., Small Manufacturing Enterprises-A Comparative Study of India and other Economics, World Bank, Oxford University Press, 1987.

Lydall, H.F. Economic Development, Asia Publishing House, 1960.

Malenbaum, W., Prospects of Indian-Development, George Allen and Unwin, London, 1961.

Mandelbaum, K. Industrialisation of Backward Area, Basil Blackwell, Oxford, 1961.

Manohar, U. Desh Pande, Entrepreneurship of Small Scale Industries, New Delhi, Deep and Deep Publications, 1982.

Mehta, M.M., Structure of Indian Industry Popular Book Depot, Bombay, 1955.

Mehta, S.S., Productivity, Production Function and Technical Change: A survey of some Indian Industries, New Delhi, Concept Publishing House, 1980.

Mehta, M.M., Structure of Industries, Bombay, Popular Book Depot, 1961.

Menon, K.S.V., Development of Backward Areas through Incentives – An Indian Experiment, New Delhi, Vidya Vahini, 1979.

Misra, S.N., and Kushal Sharma, Organisational Requirements of Village and Small Scale Industries – A case study of Alwar District of Rajasthan, Delhi, Mittal Publications, 1986.

Mohanlal, Rural Industrialisation and Regional Development, New Delhi, Deep and Deep Publications, 1987.

Muniratnam Naidu, K., "Industrial Development of Andhra Pradesh (A study in Regional Planning)" Sri Venkateswara University Press, Tirupathi).

Nau Nihal Singh, Scientific Management of Small Scale Industries, Bombay, Lalvani Publishing House, 1970.

Nannjudan, S., Economic Research for Small Industry Development. Stanford Research Institute, California, 1960.

NCAER, Survey of Backward District of Andhra Pradesh, New Delhi, 1970.

NCAER under utilisation of Industrial capacity, New Delhi 1966.

Myrdal, Gunnar, International Economy, New York, Harper and Brothers, 1956.

Pandey, T.M., Capital Structure and the Cost of Capital, Vikas Publishing House, New Delhi, 1985.

Patwardhan, V.S., Role of Small Scale Industries in the Progress of Puna and Aurangabad Districts of Maharashtra, Pune, Gokhale Institute of Politics and Economics, 1985.

Ramakrishna Sharma, "Industrial Development of Andhra Pradesh", Himalaya Publishing House, Bombay, 1982.

Ram Dawar, Institutional Finance to Small Scale Industries Hire-Purchase Finance for Plant and Machinery, New Delhi, Deep and Deep Publications, 1986.

Ramesh, P. Sinha, Some Problems of Small Scale Industry, New Delhi, Janaki Prakashan, 1985.

Rosen, George, Industrial Changes in India, Bombay, Asia Publishing House, 1957.

Robinson, E.A.C., (ed). "Backward Areas in Advanced Countries" Macmillan, 1969.

Sadak, H., Industrial Development in Backward Regions in India, Allahabad, Chugh Publication, 1986.

Sandesara, J.C., Efficacy of Incentives for Small Industries: Principal Findings of the Bombay, Hyderabad and Jaipur Surveys and Their Explanations and Implications, Bombay, Industrial Development Bank of India, 1982.

Sen, A.K., Employment, Technology and Development, Oxford Press, 1975.

Sharma, S.V.S., Small Entrepreneurial Development in Some Asian Countries—A Comparative study, New Delhi, Hight and Life Publishers, 1979.

Singh A.K., Patterns of Regional Development—A Comparative Study New Delhi, Sterling Publishers, Pvt. Ltd., 1981.

Singh N.K., Industrial Progress and Economic Growth, New Delhi, Classical Publishing Company, 1982.

Small Industry Extension Training Institute, Capital Requirements of Small Industry, Hyderabad, SIET Institute, 1974.

Stanlay, Engene and Richard Morse, Modern Small Industry for Developing Countries, New York, MC Graw Hill Book Company, 1965.

Takafusa Nakamura, Economic Development of Modern Japan, Japan, Ministry of Foreign Affairs, 1985.

Tandar, B.C., Pattern and Technique of India's Economic Development, Allahabad, Chugh Publications, 1997, Vol. 1.

Tarum, T.N.S., Small Scale Industries, and India's Economic Development, New Delhi, Deep and Deep Publications, 1986.

Tyaguneuk, O.V.L., "Industrialisation of Developing Countries" Progress Publishers, Moscow, 1973.

United Nations "Progress and Problems of Industrialisation in Underdeveloped Countries" 1955.

Upadhayaya, K.K., Financing of Industrial Growth in a Developing Region, Allahabad, Chugh Publications, 1980.

Vepa, Ram, K., Small Industry: Challenges of the Eighties, New Delhi, Vikas Publishing House, 1983.

Vepa, Ram, K., How to Succeed in Small Industry, New Delhi, Vikas Publishing House, 1984.

Visweswaraiah, Sir, M., "Prosperity through Industry".

World Bank, Employment and the Development of Small Enterprises, A Sector Policy Paper, February 1980.

World Bank, Employment and Development of Small Enterprises, Section Policy Paper, 1978.

Reports

Andhra Pradesh Industrial and Technical Consultancy Organisation Limited, Report on Rehabilitation of Sick Units in the Small Sector, APITCO, February, 1986.

Asian and Pacific Development Centre (Kualalumpur, Malaysia), Case Studies on Rural Non-Farm Activities in Kanyakumari District, Tamil Nadu and Midnapore District, West Bengal, Hyderabad, SIET Institute, May, 1984.

Asian Productivity Organisation, Productivity through Consultancy in Small Industries Enterprises, APO, Tokyo 107, Japan, 1974.

Centre for Monitoring Indian Economy, Economic Intelligence Service, Basic Statistic Relating to the Indian Economy, Bombay, Centre for Monitoring Indian Economy, September, 1989.

Development Commissioner, Small Scale Industries, Self-Employment Programme for Educated Unemployed Youth-An Evaluation Study in two Districts of Andhra Pradesh, New Delhi, Planning Commission, January, 1989.

..., All India Report on the Census of Small Scale Industries, Vol.1, New Delhi, Planning Commission, 1976.

..., Proceedings of 3rd All India District Industries Centres Conference, New Delhi, Ministry of Industry, July 15-16, 1986.

District Industries Centre, Report of the Action Plan for Industrial Development Five Year Plan (1990-93) Anantapur.

District Planning Office: The Hand Book of Statistics Anantapur District, Anantapur (1990-91).

Government of Andhra Pradesh, Statistical Abstract of Andhra Pradesh, Hyderabad, Bureau of Economics and Statistics, (1990-91).

..., Agenda Notes, Regional Conference of District Industries Centres at Vijayawada on the West; Krishna on the North and River Gundlakamma and parts of Kamma Nadu on the South.

..., Agenda Notes, State Level Conference of General Manager of District Industries Centres, Directorate of Industries, June 1982.

Government of Andhra Pradesh, Report of the Gramodaya Scheme, Prepared by Andhra Pradesh Productivity Council on behalf of Commissioner for Special Employment Scheme, Hyderabad, Commissioner of Industries, 1983.

Agenda Notes, Conference of General Managers District Industries Centres, Telangana Region, Hyderabad, Commissioner of Industries, 1984.

Guidelines for Setting up Small Scale Industries in Andhra Pradesh, Commissioner of Industries, 1984.

Report of the District Industries Centres in Andhra Pradesh, Directorate of Industries (Brief Resume 1978-79 and 1979-80).

Government of India, First Five Year Plan (1950-55), New Delhi, Planning Commission.

Government of India, First Five Year Plan (1950-55), New Delhi Planning Commission.

Report of the Village and Small Scale Industries Committee, Second Five Year Plan, New Delhi, Planning Commission.

Report of the Village and Small Scale Industries Committee, Second Five Year Plan, New Delhi, Planning Commission, October, 1955.

Fourth Five Year Plan (1969-74), New Delhi, Planning Commission.

Draft Five Year Plan (1978-83), New Delhi, Planning Commission.

Statement of Industrial Policy, New Delhi, Planning Commission, July 23, 1980.

Evaluation Study of Rural Industries Projects, New Delhi, Planning Commission (P.E.O.) 1978.

Small Scale Industries in India, Hand Book Statistics, New Delhi, 1985.

Report of the Working Group on Identification of Backward Area, New Delhi, Planning Commission.

Report of the Working Group – Fiscal and Financial Incentives for Starting Industries in Backward Areas, Development Commissioner (SSI), Ministry of Industrial Development, 1969.

Development Programme for Small Scale Industries in Backward Areas, Report of the Committee to Evolve a Strategy (Chairman, P.C. Naik) Government of India, 1976.

Government of India, First All India Workshop: General Managers of DICs, New Delhi, Development Commissioner, Small Scale Industries, 1979.

District Industries Centres: Gleanings from two Case Studies, Hyderabad, SIET Institute, February 1989.

District Industries Centre Scheme: An Overview upto January 31, 1984, New Delhi, Development Commissioner, Small Scale Industries, 1984.

Annual Survey of Industries, India for various years, New Delhi, Central Statistical Organisation.

Physical Achievements of DIC Programme (6th Plan, 1980-81 – 1984-85), An Appraisal, New Delhi, Development Commissioner (Small Scale Industries).

Government of Maharashtra, Report of the Fact Finding Committee on Regional Imbalances in Maharashtra, Bombay, July 1984.

Indian Institute of Management, Evaluation of DIC Programme in Andhra Pradesh, Bangalore, May 1988.

Industrial Development Bank of India, Reports on Development Banking in India, Bombay, (Various Years) 1982-83 to 1987-88.

International Labour Organisation (ILO), Strategies for Employment Promotion—An Evolution of Four Inter-Agency Employment Missions, Geneva, I.L.O. 1973.

Articles

Antonic Vazquez Barquero, "Small Industry in Rural Areas. The Spanish Experience Since the Beginning Economic Congress of International Economic Association, New Delhi, 1986.

Banerjee, M.K., District Industries Centres: Some Comments", Yojana, September, 16, 1978.

Banerjee, A., "Productivity Growth and Factor Substitution in Indian Manufacturing" Indian Economic Review, April 1971.

Bhalla, A.S., "Innovations and Small Producers in Developing Countries", Economic and Political Weekly, February 25, 1989, pp. M2-M14.

Bhatt, V.V., "Entrepreneurship Development: India's Experience" Finance and Development, March 1986.

Bhaumik, T.K., "Lopsided Industrial Growth—I and II", Financial Express, April 6 and 7, 1987.

Bishwanath Goldar and Vijaya Seth, "Spatial Variations in the Rate of Industrial Growth in India", Economic and Political Weekly, June 3, 1989. pp. 1237-1250.

Bognar, Jozef, "Economic Policy and Planning in Developing Countries", Akadomia Kidao, Budapest, pp. 295-296.

Bulletin, "Financing of Small Scale Industries: A Profile" Reserve Bank of India (April, 1980).

Chanery, H.B. And Tayler, L., "Development Patterns Among Countries Overtime", Review of Economics and Statistics, Nov. 1968, pp. 391-416.

Dayakar, C., "SSI's Role in Growth of Small Industries in Andhra Pradesh" Laghu Udyog Samachar, 1979 4 (2-3), pp. 39-41 and 58.

Diwan, R.K., "Returns to Scale in Indian Industry—A Comment", Indian Economic Journal, 15, 1968.

Diwan, R.K, and Gujarati, D.N., "Employment and Productivity in Indian Industries" Artha Vijnan, October 1968.

Ganapathy, V., "District Industries Centres—How they will work", Industrial India, February 1979, pp.21-22.

Habid, "Small Scale Industries Means to Eradicate Untouchability", Khadi Gramodyog (June 1975).

Jain, L.C., Development of Decentralised Industries. A Review of Some Suggestions", A review of some suggestions" Economic and Political Weekly (October 1980).

Khader Ali Khan, "Techniques of Promoting Self Employment in Urban Area", National Seminar on Promotion of Self-Employment, New Delhi, 10th November 1981.

Lakshmi Narasaiah. M, "Artisan Complexes—A strategy for rural employment generation", National Seminar on Employment Generation in Rural Sector with Focus in A.P. Sri Krishnadevaraya University, Anantapur, April 25, 1987.

Lakshmi Narasaiah. M, Technological Entrepreneurship The New Force for Economic Growth, Khadi Gramodyog, (Oct. 1997).

Morahtetz, David, "Employment Implications of Industrialisation in Developing Countries—A Survey", Economic Journal, September 1974.

Mukherji, Mukherji, 'Employment-Oriented Industries and their Role in State Economics", National Seminar on Industrialisation of States in India with Focus on Andhra Pradesh, University of Hyderabad, Aug, 7-9, 1987.

Oza, A.N., Integrated Entrepreneurship Development Programmes—The Indian Experience", Economic and Political Weekly, May, 28, 934-951.

Ojha, P.D., "Financing for Small Scale Enterprises in India" Reserve Bank of India Bulletin, RBI, Bombay, November 1982, pp. 934-951.

Pannalal, "Growth of Small Scale Units—Role of Entrepreneurial Attitudes" Laghu Udyog Samachar, 1983, pp. 11-12.

Pillai, P., "Scale and Efficiency of Small Scale Industries in India", Asian Economic Review, Vol.20, No.1, April 1978.

Parameswaran, K.P., "Some Problems of Small Scale Ancillary Industries" Productivity, Vol. 20 No. 1, April 1978.

Patil, S.M., "Prospects for Small Scale Industries During the Eighties", Bank of India Bulletin, March 1980, pp. 25-30.

..., "The Complementary Role of Small Industry in India", Man and Development, vol. 2, No.1, 1980, pp.15-21.

Pradhan H. Prasad, "Neglected Aspects of India's Development Planning" Economic and Political Weekly, July 15, 1989, pp. 1591-1595.

Pradhan, H. Prasad, "Neglected Aspedts of India's Development Planning", Economic and Political Weekly, July 15, 1989, 1951-1595.

Prassad Agarwal, "Industrialisation Thorough Small Scale Sector", The Journal of Commerce, Vol. XXXI, Part-III, No. 116, September 1978.

Prasad Bhagawan, "On Strengthening District Industries Centres" SEDME, SIET Institute, Vol. IX, No.3, September 1982, pp. 175-182.

Raghava Reddy G., "Bank Finance for Village and Small Industries". Eastern Economist (March 1981).

Rangacharya, S.S. "Employment Generation and Income Distribution Through Village and Small Industry in India: An Analytical Study: SEDME (June, 1983).

Rajuladevi, "Industrialisation Adds Key to Rural Development", Kurukshetra, December, 1984.

Ramachandran, K., 'Dynamics in Industrial Location - Location Theory Revisited", Keio Business Review, Vol. 24, No.3, Japan, Keio University, 1988.

Ramachandran, K., "Regional Incentives and Small Enterprise Location—Some International Lessons", Decision, Vol. 15, No. 1, Jan-March 1988 pp. 41-47.

Raman, C.S., "Small Industry Prospects in India", Laghu Udyog Samachar, Vol. 7, No. 3, 1982, pp. 11-12.

Alternatives to District Industries Centres" SEDME, SIET Institute, Vol. III, No. 2, June 1981, pp. 71-80.

Rangacharya, S.S., "Employment Generation and Income Distribution through Village and Small Industry in India: An Analytical Study: SEDME (June, 1983).

Rao, S.L., "Innovative Marketing Strategies: Small Enterprises Fight Large Established Companies", Economic and Political Weekly, August 26, 1989, pp. M. 127-M.130.

Rondinelli, Dennis, A., "Small Industries in Rural Development: Assessment and Perspective" Productivity, Jan-March, 1979.

Sandesara, J.C., "Employment in Industry: Seventh Plan Approach" Economic and Political Weekly, October 20-27, 1984.

Sandesara, J.C., "Small Scale Industrialisation—The Indian Experience" Economic and Political Weekly, March 26, 1988, pp. 240-654.

Shridharan, L. "Decentralisation and District Planning" The Economic Times, July 24, 1986.

Shrivastava, S.P., "A Note on the District Industries Centre Scheme, Indian Journal of Economics, Vol. LXVII, April, 1987.

Smriti Mukherji, "Employment—Oriented Industries and their Role in State Economics: 1981-82" Paper Presented at the National Seminar on Industrialisation of Indian States, University of Hyderabad, 7-9, 1987.

Sathya Sundaram, I., "DIC at the Cross-Roads", The Economic Times, December 9, 1983.

Swaminathan, M.C., "Balanced Regional Development and Incentives for Industries", SEDME, SIET Institute, Vol. V, No. 3, December 1978.

Tulpule Bagaram and R.C. Date, "Rural Wages and Productivity in Industry—A Desegregated Analysis", Economic and Political Weekly, Vol. XXIV, No. 34, August 36, 1989, pp. M.94-M.102.

Varma, R., "Employment and Production in Small Scale Industries: Some Findings of the RBI Survey", Reserve Bank of India Occasional Papers, 1980, pp. 155-166.

Vepa, Ram K., "DICs Play Effective Role in Industrialisation Sixth Plan in Retrospect" Laghu Udyog Samachar, Vol. X, No.9 April 1986, pp. 30-32.

Reports and Publications of Andhra Pradesh Government

Annual Survey of Industries, Andhra Pradesh, Bureau of Economics and Statistics.

Directory of Small Scale Units in Andhra Pradesh, Volume I, Director of Industries.

Fourth Five Year Plan, Andhra Pradesh, Draft Outline, Department of Planning and Co-operation.

Fourth Five year Plan--Outline and Programmes (1969-70 to 1973-74), Andhra Pradesh, Department of Planning and Cooperation.

Fifth Five Year Plan. Andhra Pradesh Draft Outline, Department of Planning and Cooperation.

Fifth Plan—Andhra Pradesh, Approach, Technical Papers, Planning and Cooperation Department.

Fifth Plan-Andhra Pradesh—Review of Development Technical Papers, Planning and Cooperation Department.

Industrial Estates. Exhumes for the Establishment of Assisted Industrial Estates, Department of Industries and Commerce.

Planning and Development of Backward Region, A Case Study, of Rayalaseema Volume I, Planning Land Cooperation Department, 1970.

Perspective Plan for Reyalaseema Region, Andhra Pradesh, Vol. II, Plan Programmes, Planning and Co-operation Department, 1972.

Perspective Plan for Rayalaseema Region, Andhra Pradesh, Vol. III, Methodology and detailed tables, Planning and Co-operation Department, 1974.

Report of the Annual Survey of Industries.

Sixth Five Year Plan, Andhra Pradesh Draft Outline, Department of Planning Cooperation.

Statistical abstracts for the 15 years 1970-1984, Bureau of Economics and Statistics.

Annual Reports and Memorandum and Articles

Annual Reports of Andhra Pradesh Industrial Infrastructure Corporation (APIIC) from 1973-74 to 1984-85.

Andhra Pradesh Industrial Infrastructure—A catalyst for industrial growth in Andhra Pradesh.

Annual Reports of Andhra Pradesh Industrial Development Corporation (APIDC) Limited 1976-77 to 1983-84.

APIDE, New Dimensions in Development, APIDE.

Annual Reports of Andhra Pradesh State Small Scale Industrial Development Corporation (APPSSID) from 1976-77 to 1983-84.

Annual Reports of Andhra Pradesh State Financial Corporation from 1976-77 to 1983-84.

Annual Reports of Industrial Development Bank of India, 1981-82, 1982-83.

A compendium of APSSIDC Services, Andhra Pradesh Small Scale Industrial Development Corporation.

Memorandum of Association of Andhra Pradesh Industrial Infrastructure Corporation Ltd.,

Note on Activities of APPIIC.

Other Reports

All India Report on the Census of Small Units, Development Commissioner, Small Scale Industries.

A Study of Regional Cooperation for the Fourth Plan, NCAER.

Delhi Administration, Directorate of Industries, Okhla Industrial Estate, New Delhi, 1969, p. 149.

Government of Madras, Department of Industries and Commerce, All India Seminar on Industrial Estates, Report on Proceedings, 1960.

Government of India, Small Scale Industries Board, Report of the Sub-Committee on Industrial Estates, 1960.

Industrial Policy, Administrative Staff College of India (A Course of Studies Paper).

Industrial Potential Survey of Andhra Pradesh—Report of a Study Team—Sponsored by the IDBI-RBI, IFCI and APSFC.

Industrial Development of Backward Areas, Industrial Development Bank of India.

Report on IDBI Assisted Industrial Estates in Karnataka and Andhra Pradesh, Industrial Development Bank of India, 1980.

Study Group on Industrial Estates in Maharashtra, Bombay, 1966, p.

Survey of Backward Districts of Andhra Pradesh National Council for Applied Economic Research (NCAER) New Delhi, 1970.

Techno Economic Surveys of the States of India, NCAER.

Index

R

S